WHAT'S
BOTHERING
RASHI?

A GUIDE TO
IN-DEPTH ANALYSIS OF
HIS TORAH COMMENTARY

WHAT'S BOTHERING RASHI?

A GUIDE TO
IN-DEPTH ANALYSIS OF
HIS TORAH COMMENTARY

AVIGDOR BONCHEK

VAYIKRA

FOCUS ON RASHI'S USE OF MIDRASH

JERUSALEM FELDHEIM PUBLISHERS NEW YORK

Published in collaboration with
Be'er HaTorah Institute

First published 2000
ISBN 1-58330-400-2

FELDHEIM PUBLISHERS
POB 35002, Jerusalem, Israel 91350
200 Airport Executive Park, Nanuet, N.Y. 10954

www.feldheim.com

Printed in Israel

Designed & Produced by:
Laser Pages Publishing Ltd., Jerusalem
972-2-652-2226

10 9 8 7 6 5 4 3 2 1

שמואל קמנצקי
Rabbi S. Kamenetsky

2018 Upland Way
Philadelphia, Pa 19131

Home: 215-473-2798
Study: 215-473-1212

בעזהשי"ת יום ג' פ' בשלח חמ"ש לפ"ק יקח לבבו

לעלין ובימו ההביה ד' לבריאה ד'שפ"ק אשר

אחרי ברכת שלום הרבים כנפשם.

קבלתי התלק של אגרת כתבים של שולחן להוריות

לאור. ועיינין שמעלא חיים טבל פברי דלו לשמת שלול

עברי הגל.

נכו כותב של הראשונים שדבריהם כפטיר ומלא סלע

וכל גידול ומדרגה עודן לכל שיש לעי כתורה ומל. שיש

כלל ושלא שבדרוש של בדרו רכן של ירוש רש"י של

וכל ככה להתנרש היינהם.

ויבנה כח להתחזק לאלאור לא המלמד של תתא

תואשי נגרה שולל ומעוק של נכן.

ואני מופר מעדר דולל מדות שלרלן

הק' שמואל דרן.

דולרי בן ה

Rabbi Nachman Bulman

Yeshivat Ohr Somayach

Ohr Lagolah

הרב נחמן בולמן

ישיבת אור שמח

אור לגולה

בס״ד

מוצש״ק אור ליום א׳ א׳ דר״ח אדר א׳ תש״ס פה עה״ק ת״ו

February 5, 2000

It is a privilege to write a few words of approbation in honor of R. Avigdor Bonchek's third work on Rashi — Vayikra.

R. Bonchek's first two works have won wide approval and undoubtedly the newest work will win even wider appreciation. The expansion of Torah learning in our time has made R. Bonchek's work especially needed and welcome.

On one hand, Rashi is the Master Teacher of all Israel in every area of Torah and particularly in Chumash. Yet, for all his clarity, his subtlety causes many in our times to lack genuine understanding of what he is saying.

What are the lines of distinction in Rashi between P'shat and Drash? How does Rashi "use" Midrash to deepen our understanding of the deeper P'shat? Avigdor Bonchek deftly illuminates Rashi's meaning and takes us into his laboratory and methodology, in a striking manner and with precious insight. Especially does Vayikra require such "opening up" of Rashi. Many will be grateful to R. Bonchek for his effort.

הכותב לכ׳ התורה׳ לכ׳ רש״י הקדוש, רבן של ישראל ולכ׳ מפיצי ומסבירי תורתו,

Nachman Bulman נחמן בולמן

נחמן בולמן

ירושלים עיה״ק ת״ו

137/21 Ma'alot Daphna, Jerusalem 97762 Israel • Tel: 02-824321 :טל • 97762 ירושלים 137\21 מעלות דפנה

INSTITUTE FOR
THE STUDY OF
R A S H I
AND EARLY TORAH COMMENTARIES

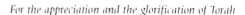

For the appreciation and the glorification of Torah

The Institute for the Study of Rashi and Early Commentaries is proud to present this, the third volume of the *"What's Bothering Rashi?"* series. This volume continues the tradition of analyzing, in easily understandable language and in a clearly reasoned fashion, the methods of learning *Rashi* and other Torah commentaries, in depth.

The goals of the Institute include the completion of this series but also go beyond this achievement. We hope to complete the series itself, G-d willing, within the next two years. At the same time, we are preparing school-level workbooks with a detailed teacher's manual that will make the teaching of the Torah and its classic commentaries an exciting and intellectually challenging classroom experience in Torah study. We also plan on producing audiocassettes for individual adult study.

These works are to be translated into Hebrew for the non-English reading public.

The purpose of the Institute is to make available to the Torah community, both student and adult, both neophyte and scholar, the wonders of in-depth study of the Written Torah. *Chumash-and-Rashi* has been the foundation of Torah study for generations of Jews. Quite commonly, however, the special techniques necessary to engage the student to think on his own, have not been emphasized. The ability to apply one's innate analytical powers to grasp the inner logic of the commentator's message has not received sufficient consideration. In such cases, the student has been deprived of the exhilarating experience of viewing the Torah through the eyes of our classic Torah commentators. The question-and-answer method of learning, so essential to a deep understanding of Rashi, is likewise crucial to a better appreciation of all the classical Torah commentaries. The emphasis of all the works of the Institute, present and planned, is to guide the student in a method of self-discovery which will enable him to proceed in his learning to achieve a constantly expanding appreciation of the wisdom and beauty of our Written Torah.

Sincerely,

Avigdor Bonchek

Avigdor Bonchek, Ph.D.
Director

2 Wisconsin Circle, Suite 700, Chevy Chase, Maryland 20815 Tel: (301) 656-5540

— CONTENTS —

Acknowledgments

מודה אני

This is the third volume of the *"What's Bothering Rashi?"* series. The last piece of work in the preparation of these volumes is the "Acknowledgments." It is a pleasant task because it means that the hard work has been completed and all that remains is to thank those who have helped in this inspiring work. After many months of working on this manuscript, I am reminded that the final product was not achieved by me alone. The support, both intellectual and emotional, that I have had all the way through, from family and friends, has been indispensable.

I ask forgiveness from any reader who has memorized the Acknowledgments from the previous volumes! Because, I repeat myself. But then we repeat מודה אני each day of our lives, because each day we have what to be grateful for. So too, I again thank everyone who has continued to help me. These include my wife, Shulamis and our children, each of whom has helped me in this work in so many ways — intellectual stimulation, the give and take of Torah discussion, encouragement and love.

For the past year I have attended a *Parashat Hashavua* study group lead by Dr. Gavriel Cohen in Jerusalem. The excellent teachers and lively discussions of the group offered much insight into both Rashi and the ways of the *midrash.* I am indebted to the participants for creating the right ambience in which we gained a deeper understanding and appreciation of *Hashem's* Timeless Torah.

Since the publication of our last volume, we have formed "The Institute for the Study of Rashi and Early Torah Commentaries." To my colleagues in the Institute I owe a particular debt of gratitude for their encouragement and advice all the way through the preparation of this work.

The preparation and publication of this volume was made possible by a grant from the Memorial Foundation for Jewish Culture.

My deepest gratitude is to *Hashem* for offering me the opportunity to contribute my portion in His Torah. He made it possible for me and my family to live in Eretz Yisrael and living in Eretz Yisrael has been most conducive to the creation of this work. I don't think that I would have embarked on such an endeavor had I remained in the U.S. I think, for the most part, I would have followed my professional leanings in the practice of psychology and would have been a passive participant in the study of Torah. But, as anyone who lives here knows, living passively in Israel is an oxymoron. Fortunately my Israeli "activism" took the form of ongoing "conversations" with the classic Torah commentators. For all this I am grateful.

It is my hope that this volume will be of benefit to everyone who loves the study of Torah. Those who strive to uncover its manifold meanings, its spiritual lessons and its moral and ethical teachings. Understanding Rashi's ever-fascinating commentary in all its depth, is a fitting starting point on that breathtaking journey.

Avigdor Bonchek
Jerusalem, 5760

A FORE WORD _____

This volume, *What's Bothering Rashi? Vayikra*, is the third of a planned five-volume work on Rashi's Torah commentary. The purpose of these books is to illustrate a method of analysis of Rashi's commentary that enables the student to derive the maximum meaning from his exquisitely concise commentary. The *Bereishis* volume offered many examples of Rashi's basic exegetic style. The *Shemos* volume continued with more illuminating examples with a particular focus on disputes between Rashi and Ramban. In this way the student could get a taste of the different styles of interpretation of these two Torah giants.

In this volume we have focused on Rashi's use of *midrash*. Examining Rashi's creative inclusion of *midrash* in his commentary sheds additional light on his original interpretive methods. As an introduction to this topic I have included a chapter which delineates Rashi's various uses of *midrash*.

It is our hope that the completed five volume set of *"What's Bothering Rashi?"* will offer the student an all-inclusive view of Rashi's many-faceted commentary.

One last word before you begin. The book of *Vayikra* is a book of laws, the subject matter is more difficult than most of what we have dealt with in *Bereishis* and *Shemos*. As a consequence, Rashi's commentary will be more difficult. I hope we have presented it in a way that will make it accessible to all students.

Rashi and His Way with *Midrash*

וַיִּשְׁמְעוּ. יש מדרשי אגדה רבים וכבר סדרום רבותינו על מכונם
בבראשית רבה ובשאר מדרשות, ואני לא באתי אלא לפשוטו
של מקרא ולאגדה המיישבת דברי המקרא דבר דבר על אפניו.
(בראשית ג:ח)

They heard: *Rashi*: There are many Aggadic *midrashim*
and our Rabbis have already organized them in their
proper order in *Bereishis Rabbah* and in other *midrashim*.
But I have come only to give the Plain Meaning of the
Scriptures (*p'shuto shel mikra*) and the Aggada which
serves to clarify the words of the Scriptures in a way which
fits in with them. (Genesis 3:8)

RASHI: *P'SHAT* AND *DRASH*

The above quote from Rashi's Torah commentary serves as the only
prologue to his classic Torah commentary. In his characteristically brief
style, he tells us his guidelines for this commentary. This quote is the
source of the well established belief that Rashi is essentially a *p'shat*
commentator, for does he not say "But I have come only to give the
p'shuto shel mikra"?

Yet, in spite of this, more than 70% of Rashi's Torah commentary has its
source in the *midrashim* and the Talmud. In view of this, Rashi's reliance on *midrash* can neither be denied nor should it be underestimated.
But if Rashi draws most of his comments from the *midrash*, what about
his claim that he has "come only to give the *p'shuto shel mikra*"? And,
on the other hand, if he does use *midrash* to such a large extent, does that
mean that his commentary is no more than an anthology of the Sages'
sage *midrashic* comments?

There is no consensus among scholars as to the answers to these questions. But I will try to give a fair, though somewhat simplified, answer
to each of them.

First of all, Rashi's claim to deal only with *p'shat* is modified by himself in this comment itself. For he continues and says: "and with such *aggados* that explain the words of the Scriptures in a manner that fits in with them."

Rashi is saying, in effect, that his purpose is to explain the Torah according to *p'shat*, but that he will *also* turn to *midrashim* if they can be seen to accord with the words of the text. It is this second half of his comment that interests us here. He clearly says that he will use *midrash* in his commentary. Are his comments which are based on *midrash* also to be considered *p'shat* interpretation? This is an open question. There are three main views on this question. We will list them without entering into the debate in depth.

1) One view is that all *midrashim* in Rashi's commentary are in the service of *p'shat*. All of Rashi's comments, *midrashim* and others, are thus considered to be *p'shat*.

2) Another opinion is that many, perhaps most, *midrashim* cited by Rashi, while not literally *p'shat*, are never-the-less grounded in the words of the verse. In these cases the text has certain "irregularities," anomalies or nuances that raise questions which need to be explained. The *midrashic* interpretation serves to give meaning to these "irregularities." But this does not necessarily mean that such interpretations are *p'shat*. Perhaps they fall somewhere between pure *p'shat* and outright *drash*. This view would seem to be closest to what Rashi says above when he adds: "*Aggados* that explain the words of the Scriptures in a manner that fits in with them."

3) One last view is that Rashi may cite a *midrash* for its educational/moral/religious lesson without it necessarily being in any way part and parcel of a *p'shat* interpretation; it may not even have any "anchor" in the words of the Torah (as do those in #2 above).

Among the Rashi comments we analyze in this volume, we will see a variety of examples some which may be supportive of one or another of the above views. My personal view is that the vast majority of Rashi's comments follow #2 above, though some may fall into category #3.

One other point should be made. The term *p'shat* itself is not a clearly defined concept. It would seem that Rashi's view of *p'shat* differs from that of the Rashbam, Joseph Bechor Shor or the Ramban, to name a few of the classical commentators. These Rishonim view *p'shat* in a way similar to the way we ordinarily do, i.e., interpretations based on grammar, syntax and context. While Rashi's view of *p'shat* is highly influenced by the Sages' view, over context. (See the Shemos volume of *"What's Bothering Rashi?"* pages 136ff.)

In summary: Rashi's commentary can be said to be a blend of outright *p'shat* together with a weaving of *midrash* which has some anchor in the words of the Torah-text.

RASHI'S COMMENTARY: NOT A *MIDRASHIC* ANTHOLOGY

We also asked: Is Rashi's inclusion of *midrashim* in his commentary just a compilation of those interesting interpretations of the Sages?

The answer is unequivocal: No! Rashi is not an anthologist of *midrashim*. As he said, the Rabbis have already done this in *Bereishis Rabbah* and other *midrashim*. One of the most fascinating and intellectually challenging aspects of learning Rashi is to see how he uses the *midrash* and attempting to understand the way he uses it. Rashi does not just "paste" a *midrash* into his commentary. He frequently makes changes; he may select among several *midrashim*; he may splice a *midrash* taking parts of it while deleting other parts; he may edit, changing or adding his own words; and he may transfer a *midrash* from the verse it is attached to in the source and move it to a different verse. *In short, Rashi's use of midrash is a very creative and original exercise in commentary.* In this volume we will be interested in closely examining some examples of this creative aspect of Rashi's unique contribution to Torah commentary. In each sedra we will analyze at least one such Rashi-comment.

A BRIEF INTRODUCTION TO *MIDRASH*

Some introductory remarks about the *midrash* should be helpful here.

The literature of the Talmudic period (*circa* 100 BCE–500 CE) can be divided into two main bodies of work:

1) Talmud (Babylonian and Jerusalem) which consists of *mishna*, *beraisos*, and *gemora*.

2) The *Midrashim*, divided into two types: *midrash-halacha* and *midrash-aggada*.

THE TALMUD

The early Sages (100 BCE–200 CE), called the *Tanaim*, are the Sages who are quoted in the *mishna*. These include such individuals as Hillel the Elder, Rabbis Yochanan Ben Zakai, Gamliel, Yishmael, Akiva, Shimon ben Yochai, to name a few. These Sages lived and taught in Eretz Yisroel.

The *mishna* was edited and finalized by Rabbi Yehuda Hanasi in Eretz Yisroel around the year 200 CE. This became the basis for intensive study, discussion and debate in the study halls of Eretz Yisroel and Babylonia. The Sages who discussed and clarified the meaning of the *mishna* and other Tanaic sayings are referred to as the *Amoraim*. They are the ones quoted in the Gemora. These include such individuals as Rav Yochanan, Reish Lakish, Rav, Shmuel, Abaya and Rava. The Talmud (*mishna* plus *gemora*) contains many *midrashic* interpretations.

Midrash: A Definition

Definition: *Midrash*, in its broadest sense, are interpretations of verses in the Tanach by the Sages of the Talmudic period. This may surprise some students. They may have thought of *midrash* as a particular type of interpretation (*drash*) which is different from, and opposed, to *p'shat*. This assumption is only partially true. It is true that in Rashi's commentary he will often give us *p'shat* then he will offer a *midrash*. Which means that, in Rashi's terminology, the two are not identical. But while this is generally true, it is not always so, even in Rashi's view. See, for example, our analysis of Leviticus 4:3 where Rashi uses *aggada* for *p'shat*.

But the definition given above is true in the sense that the *midrashim* are made up of a variety of different types of interpretations, not just *drash*. They cover the whole spectrum of PARDES, *p'shat, remez, drash*, and *sode*.

Keeping this defintion in mind, let us look at the types of *midrashic* compilations that exist. They can be divided into two types: *midrash-halacha* and *midrash-aggada*.

Midrash Halacha

Midrash-halacha are the halachic (legal) discussions of the *Tanaim* of Eretz Yisroel. They are similar to the Talmudic discussions, in that they are records of halachic discourse by the same *Tanaim* whose names appear both in the mishna and in these midrashim. The *midrash-halacha* compilations consist of the following books.

   Mechilta on the book of Shemos;
   Toras Cohanim (also known as *Sifra*) on the book of Vayikra;
   Sifri on the two books of Bamidbar and Devarim.

There is no *midrash-halacha* on Bereishis since that book has very few mitzvos and thus little material to discuss in a halachic way.

The main difference between the Talmud and these *midrashim* is that the latter follow the books and sedras of the Torah, while the Talmud follows the order of the *mishna* as arranged by Rabbi Yehuda Hanasi.

MIDRASH-HALACHA VS HALACHA

Midrash-halacha and *halacha* are not the same thing. *Midrash* means, as we said, lessons learned from analyzing the Scriptural text. All halacha derived in this way are *midrash-halacha*. But there are laws that are not derived from the words of the Torah or Prophets. These are called *Halacha l'Moshe m'Sinai* "laws given to Moses at Sinai." An example of such a law is the regulation that all teffilin must be black. This is a halacha which has no roots in the written Torah, nevertheless it has the same weight as laws that are derived from the text.

MIDRASH-AGGADA

The other catagory of *midrash* compilation is *midrash-aggada*, it is mainly non-legal discussions (moral, religious lessons) of the *Tanaim* and *Amoraim* (200-500 CE) compiled in Eretz Yisroel. The main one is *Midrash Rabbah* which covers the Five Books of the Torah and the five megillos. Also in this catagory are the *Tanchuma*, *Pirkei D'Rebbi Eliezer* and *Yalkut Shimonie*.

MIDRASH-AGGADA VS AGGADA

As *midrash-halacha* and *halacha* are not identical, so too, *midrash-aggada* and *aggada* are not one and the same. *Midrash-aggada* is any moral, religious or ethical lesson that can be derived from verses in the Scriptures. *Aggada*, on the other hand, are any such lessons that are not derived from the Scriptures. A good example is the following from tractate *Shabbos* 31a.

> "The Rabbis learned: An incident with a gentile who came to Shamai and said to him: 'How many Torahs do you have?' Shamai answered him 'Two. The Written Torah and the Oral Torah.' The gentile said: 'Regarding the Written Torah I believe you, but regarding the Oral Torah I do not believe you. Convert me on the condition that you teach me (only) the Written Torah.' Shamai yelled at him and threw him out with a rebuke. The gentile came to Hillel and he converted him. (He began teaching him). On the

first day he taught him א, ב, ג, ד. The next day Hillel taught him (the sounds of these letters) in just the opposite way (e.g. Hillel said an א was a ד). The gentile protested 'Yesterday you said differently!' Hillel answered him: 'Do you not rely on me (to teach you the correct reading)? Then you can also rely on me that there is an Oral Torah as well."

This *aggada* has no basis in the words of the Written Torah, and therefore it is not a *midrash-aggada*. Of course this *aggada* is central to the very idea of *midrash-aggada* because the issue discussed is precisely that the Written Torah is invalid without the accompaniment of the Oral Torah (*midrashim*). I like this particular *aggada* because of its profound message. Shamai and Hillel and all traditional Jews claim that these two Torahs are inseparable. In order to hammer this point home, Hillel, ingeniously showed the gentile that there is no such thing as a written text without an oral tradition which accompanies it. He made his point by showing that even the foundation of the written tradition, the alphabet, cannot be learned without a teacher who teaches its vocalization orally. Even moreso is the Oral Torah necessary to gain a fuller understanding of the Written Torah's meaning.

RASHI AND HIS USE OF *MIDRASH*

Rashi, who wrote a running commentary on the Babylonian Talmud, was familiar with the *midrashim* found therein. He was also knowledgeable of the compilations of aggadic *midrashim* like *Midrash Rabbah*, *Tanchuma*, and the halachic *midrashim* like *Mechilta*, *Toras Cohanim* and *Sifri*. It has been suggested that for each of the five books of the Torah, Rashi had a "favorite" *midrash* that he used as the main, though not exclusive, source for his commentary for each of the different books of the Torah. On his commentary to Bereishis it is *Bereishis Rabbah*; to Shemos it is *Mechilta*; to Vayikra it is *Toras Cohanim*; to Bamidbar and Devarim it is *Sifri*.

THE VARIOUS WAYS RASHI USES *MIDRASH*

As we said above, Rashi's use of *midrash* entails more than just quoting a *midrash*. Many times he makes changes from the original *midrashic* source. It is of more than passing interest to understand why he makes such changes. If we are able to understand this, we can gain invaluable insight into Rashi's way of thinking. Rashi was a very clear headed and rational thinker, as is evident from an analysis of his commentary. Learning to understand what he says is a great accomplishment; learning to think as he did, is a prodigious achievement. Applying this skill in the study of Torah, opens up doors to a deeper understanding of the multiple layers of meaning in the Torah's words.

We will examine and illustrate some of the different ways Rashi relates to and changes the *midrash* that he uses in his commentary.

This includes:

I. Selecting one *midrash* from among many.

II. Changing the location of the *midrash*.

III. Changing the wording of the *midrash*.

IV. Combining two separate *midrashim*.

V. Rejecting a *midrash*.

VI. Rashi relates to Torah-text; *midrash* relates to its ideas.

I. Rashi Selects One *Midrash* from Among Many _____

As we said, Rashi may select a particular *midrash* from among many. In this volume we will see several examples of this. See, for example, Rashi's comment to Leviticus 10:1, 19:14 and 26:42. And in the Shemos volume of "*What's Bothering Rashi?*"on Exodus 13:17. Rashi's choice is usually determined by such factors as context — the *midrash* that best blends in with the context will be preferred as will the *midrash* that best makes sense of an unusual wording in the Torah.

Following is an illustrative example of Rashi's technique of choosing one of several *midrashim*. This is from Genesis and was suggested by my son, Chanoch.

Genesis 27:1

וַיְהִי כִּי־זָקֵן יִצְחָק וַתִּכְהֶיןָ עֵינָיו מֵרְאֹת וַיִּקְרָא אֶת־עֵשָׂו וגו׳

וַתִּכְהֶיןָ. בעשנן של אלו שהיו מעשנות ומקטירות לעבודה זרה. דבר אחר: כדי שיטול יעקב את הברכות.

His [eyesight] became dim: *Rashi*: Because of the smoke of these (women) who would burn incense for idol worship; another explanation: To enable Jacob to receive the blessings.

Rashi chose two explanations for Isaac's blindness, which derive from the *midrash*. The second can easily be seen as *p'shat*, even though its source is the *midrash*. But what is relevant for us is that there are at least three other *midrashic* explanations of this verse which Rashi did not choose.

> 1) When Isaac was bound on the altar for slaughter ...the ministering angels cried and their tears fell upon his eyes and as a result his eyesight dimmed. (*Bereishis Rabbah*)

This *midrash* is also found in most printed *chumashim* of the Rashi-comment to this verse, but it is probably an error. The first printing of Rashi (in the city of Reggio di Calabria, Italy in 1475), an authoritative text, this *midrash* does not appear in Rashi's comment.

In the tractate *Megilla* 28a we find the following two *midrashim*.

> 2) " Rav Eliezer said: The eyes of one who looks at an evil person will become dimmed as it says 'And it was when Isaac grew old and his eyes became dim from seeing...'" because he looked at the evil Esau, this is what caused it.

> 3) Rav Yitzchak said: One should never make light of a curse of an ordinary person because Avimelech cursed Sarah which was fulfilled in her offspring (Isaac) as it says 'Behold this is for you for a covering of the eyes' (Genesis 26:16).

Rashi was aware of these *midrashim*, nevertheless he chose not to use them for his commentary on this verse. Why? And why did he choose the ones he did use?

"Aggados That Clarify the Words of the Scriptures"

The two *midrashim* that Rashi chose have a reasonable connection to the context within which this verse finds itself. The first *midrash* refers to Esau's wives; they had just been mentioned in the previous verse, as causing Isaac and Rebecca bitterness. The second *midrash* shows how Isaac's blindness is a lead-in to the story that follows, about the stealing of the blessings. This was only possible because Isaac was blind and couldn't distinguish between Jacob and Esau.

The *midrashim* which were not used by Rashi, on the other hand, have nothing to do with the context of the verse nor with its wording. This is what Rashi meant when he said (Genesis 3:8) he would use the aggada when "it serves to clarify the words of the Scriptures..." And, we would add, he would not include *midrashim* that do not serve this function. It is important to remember this. Rashi always chooses and selects when he includes a *midrash* in his commentary. With this rule in mind, we can better understand why he chose a particular *midrash* and its relevance.

II. Rashi Changes the Location of a *Midrash* _____

Another example of Rashi's creative use of *midrash* is when he cites a *midrash* from one verse but applies it to a different verse. This is not an unusual occurrence in his commentary. It is always a challenge to understand why he makes this transfer.

Following is a clear example of this type of change which can be found in Rashi's commentary on Genesis.

Eliezer was sent to find a wife for his master, Abraham's, son, Isaac. As he retells Rebecca's family the conversation he had with Abraham before he left, he says the following:

Genesis 24:39

וָאֹמַר אֶל־אֲדֹנִי אֻלַי לֹא־תֵלֵךְ הָאִשָּׁה אַחֲרָי.

אֻלַי לֹא תֵלֵךְ הָאִשָּׁה. אֻלַי כְּתִיב בַּת הָיְתָה לוֹ לֶאֱלִיעֶזֶר וְהָיָה
מְחַזֵּר לִמְצוֹא עִילָה שֶׁיֹּאמַר לוֹ אַבְרָהָם לִפְנוֹת אֵלָיו לְהַשִּׂיאוֹ בִּתּוֹ,
אָמַר לוֹ אַבְרָהָם בְּנִי בָּרוּךְ וְאַתָּה אָרוּר וְאֵין אָרוּר מִדַּבֵּק בְּבָרוּךְ.
Perhaps the woman will not go: *Rashi:* It is written אֻלַי (not אוּלַי). Eliezer had a daughter and was looking for an excuse so that Abraham should tell him that he is turning to him to allow his (Eliezer's) daughter to marry (Isaac). Abraham said to him: 'My son is blessed and you are cursed. One who is cursed cannot cleave to one who is blessed.'

Rashi's *Midrashic* Source

Rashi's source is found in *Bereishis Rabbah*, but with some differences:

1) This *midrash* is found on an earlier verse (Genesis 24:5) where Eliezer is speaking with Abraham. Our verse is a retelling of that conversation when Eliezer is speaking with Rebecca's family.

2) The *midrash* does not make a point of the spelling of the word אלי, which Rashi does. Rashi says, in effect, that since the word, which is pronounced אוּלַי, is spelled here without the ו, it could be read as אֵלַי meaning "to me." This, for Rashi, is the basis of the *drash* that Eliezer hoped that Abraham would turn to him ("to me"). But it is not the basis for the *midrash* in *Bereishis Rabbah*, because the *midrash* relates to verse 24:5 where the word is spelled אוּלַי, complete with the ו.

Rashi has moved the *midrash* from 24:5 to 24:39.

Two questions can be asked regarding Rashi's change of location:

>   1) Why did Rashi not comment on the first verse, as the *midrash* did? and
>
>   2) Why did he comment and use the *midrash* on this verse?

UNDERSTANDING RASHI'S REASON FOR THE TRANSFER

Rashi certainly made this change intentionally. We can only speculate as to the reason. But it would seem that Rashi needed the *midrash* to explain the unusual spelling of the word אלי. This is what was bothering him and the *midrash* afforded an explanation of this anomaly. The *midrash* in *Bereishis Rabbah* itself, on the other hand, was not concerned with the strange spelling, it was giving us an interpretation of the original (24:5) verse. There Eliezer used the word אולי which means "perhaps" but this word is used when one hopes something good will happen, "perchance." But, since he was telling Abraham that maybe things won't work out as his master had wanted, it would have been correct to use the word פן, which means "lest" and is appropriate when forecasting an unwanted event. This is the basis for the *midrash* and therefore it commented at the first opportunity, which was on verse 24:5.

We see that the goals of *midrash* and the goals of Rashi, as Torah commentator, are not always identical. Because of these different purposes, the *midrash* and Rashi each made use of this interpretation on different verses, each to suit his own particular goal.

III. RASHI CHANGES THE WORDING OF THE *MIDRASH* _____

Sometimes Rashi will quote a *midrash* but in the process will change a word or two of the *midrash*'s original wording. Some might attribute this slight change to a lapse of memory on Rashi's part. We disagree with this easy answer, for the following reasons. For one, Rashi in his comprehensive Talmud commentary also quotes other Talmudic texts and *midrashim*. In that commentary he always quotes them precisely. It is not reasonable that he would be less precise in his Torah commentary. For another reason, Rashi can quote a *midrash* precisely but change just a word or two. Such selective "forgetting" is not reasonable. And finally, when we investigate these apparent "lapses of memory" we discover that there is method behind them. It is then that we realize how Rashi has applied his creative touch to his *midrash*-based comments.

An example of this can be found in this volume in our analysis of Leviticus 26:8 in *Parashas Bechukosai*.

We will take another example of this type of change from a well known Rashi-comment that has become part of our daily language.

Exodus 19:2

וַיִּסְעוּ מֵרְפִידִים וַיָּבֹאוּ מִדְבַּר סִינַי וַיַּחֲנוּ בַּמִּדְבָּר וַיִּחַן־שָׁם יִשְׂרָאֵל נֶגֶד הָהָר.

וַיִּחַן שָׁם יִשְׂרָאֵל. כְּאִישׁ אֶחָד בְּלֵב אֶחָד, אֲבָל שְׁאָר כָּל הַחֲנִיּוֹת בְּתַרְעוּמוֹת וּבְמַחֲלוֹקֶת.

And Israel encamped there: *Rashi*: As one man with one heart. But all other encampments were done in a murmuring and in dissension.

RASHI'S *MIDRASHIC* SOURCE

The *Mechilta* has the following *midrash*:

> "**And Israel encamped there**: Wherever it says 'and *they* journeyed', 'and *they* encamped', it indicates that they were journeying with dissension and they were encamping with dissension. But here it says 'and Israel encamped (in the singular) there' indicating that were *all of one heart*."

Do you see any difference between the wording in the *midrash* and Rashi's wording?

There are several differences. But what is crucial is that the *midrash* says "with one heart" while Rashi says "as one man, with one heart ." Rashi added the words, "as one man" which do not appear in the *midrash*, it is Rashi's own, original, phrase.

This is not unintentional. For if we look at another well known Rashi-comment we find a similar word change.

Exodus 14:10

וּפַרְעֹה הִקְרִיב וַיִּשְׂאוּ בְנֵי־יִשְׂרָאֵל אֶת־עֵינֵיהֶם וְהִנֵּה מִצְרַיִם נֹסֵעַ אַחֲרֵיהֶם וַיִּירְאוּ מְאֹד וַיִּצְעֲקוּ בְנֵי־יִשְׂרָאֵל אֶל־ה׳.

נֹסֵעַ אַחֲרֵיהֶם. בְּלֵב אֶחָד כְּאִישׁ אֶחָד.

He (Egypt) traveled after them. *Rashi*: With one heart, as one man.

The *midrashic* source for this is also in the *Mechilta*.

> **"He (Egypt) traveled after them**. It does not say '*were* traveling' (plural) but '*was* traveling' (singular). This tells us that the Egyptians all formed squadrons, each (marching) *as one man*."

Again we find the strange phenomenon, Rashi expands on the words of the *midrash*. The *midrash* has only "as one man," Rashi has "With one heart, as one man." He had turned a simple two-word explanation into a memorable aphorism.

Once we see Rashi's *midrashic* sources we can understand the answer to a question that has puzzled many students. The question has been asked: Why did Rashi switch the words in these two quotes; in one he has "with one heart, as one man" and in the other he has "as one man, with one heart" ? This seems quite arbitrary. But when see the *midrash* on which these quotes are based, we can understand. The Egyptian army was waging a battle against the Israelites. Manly strength was the important factor. There the *midrash* says "as one man." When the Israelites stood at Mt. Sinai, on the other hand, spirituality, matters of the heart, were central. There the *midrash* says "with one heart."

Rashi added his own touch by poetizing these simple terms. He strengthened the *midrash*'s words and bolstered them by adding two words. To the *midrash*'s "As one man". he added "*With one hear*t as one man." To the *midrash*'s "with one heart" he added "*As one man* with one heart." With this slight emendation Rashi has transformed the *midrash*'s phrase into a popular proverb.

IV. RASHI COMBINES TWO *MIDRASHIM*

It is a very frequent occurrence for Rashi to offer two interpretations, one *p'shat* and one *drash* on a particular verse. Less frequent, but also typical, is the case where Rashi will offer two interpretations, both from the *midrash* and combine them into one comment. An example of this can be found in this volume on the analysis of Rashi's comment to Leviticus 14:4. In such cases we must understand why Rashi combines two *midrashim* and what, if any, connection there is between the two.

The following is an example from Gensis 33:14.

יַעֲבָר־נָא אֲדֹנִי לִפְנֵי עַבְדּוֹ וַאֲנִי אֶתְנַהֲלָה לְאִטִּי לְרֶגֶל הַמְּלָאכָה
אֲשֶׁר־לְפָנַי וּלְרֶגֶל הַיְלָדִים עַד אֲשֶׁר־אָבֹא אֶל־אֲדֹנִי שֵׂעִירָה.

עד אשר אבא אל אדני שעירה. הרחיב לו הדרך שלא היה
דעתו ללכת אלא עד סוכות. אמר, אם דעתו לעשות לי רעה
ימתין עד בואי אצלו (עבודה זרה כה:) והוא לא הלך, ואימתי
ילך? בימי המשיח שנאמר ועלו מושעים בהר ציון לשפוט את
הר עשו (ב"ר עז: יד). ומדרשי אגדה יש לפרשה זו רבים.

Until I come to my lord at Seir: *Rashi*: He mentioned a
much longer journey for him (when he said he would come
to Seir) for he intended to go only until Succoth. He reasoned: 'If Esau intends to do me harm, let him wait until
I come to him.' But he did not go. When will he go ? In
the days of the Messiah, as it says "And the saviors shall
go up on Mt Zion to judge Mt. Esau." There are many
midrashic explanations of this section.

Rashi has combined two different *midrashim* here. The first from the
Talmud *Avodah Zarah* 25b tells us that Jacob intentionally misled Esau
in order to protect himself. The second *midrash* is from *Bereishis Rabbah*
which tells us that Jacob will, in fact, fulfill his pledge to come to Seir,
but only in the End of Days.

Why does Rashi combine these two, apparently contradictory, *midrashim*,
one which says that Jacob lied to Esau with another which says that he
prophesied truthfully. The *Maharsha* explains that while Jacob certainly
was not honest with his brother Esau, nevertheless, Rashi wanted to find
some truth in Jacob's words. He did a similar thing in his comment to
Jacob's words to his father Isaac "I am Esau your first born." (Genesis
27:19). This is why he added the *midrash* about Jacob coming to Esau in
the days of the Messiah.

"THERE ARE MANY *MIDRASHIM* TO THIS SECTION"

Rashi's last words in this comment are most puzzling and fascinating.
He adds "and there are many *midrashim* to this section." This kind of
statement is not unusual for Rashi. Many times he will refer to *midrashim*
and yet not cite them explicitly. This usually means that he rejects them
as *p'shat*. But what is strange in this case is that Rashi says "there are
many *midrashim*." Yet when we look into *Bereishis Rabbah* (Rashi's
main *midrashic* source) and other *midrashic* compilations we don't find
any other *midrashim*, except the ones Rashi cited! Also in the Talmud
we find no other *midrashim* on this verse other than the one Rashi offers

in the first half of this comment. Very strange indeed. There are no other *midrashim* except the ones Rashi mentions and yet he says "there are many"!

An answer to this puzzle has been suggested by Rav Yigal Shaffran.

When we look at the Talmudic source that Rashi quotes we find that it discusses the laws of safe conduct when in the presence of an idol worshiper.

> "He (the Jew) should not be alone with him (the pagan). If they are going up (a mountain) or going down, the Jew should not be below while the pagan is above....If he asks where he is going he should lengthen the journey just as Jacob our father did with Esau as it says "until I come to my master to Seir."

Is it possible that Rashi surreptitiously drew our attention to these laws without mentioning them openly? Rashi lived in Northern Europe during a period of violent anti-Semitic provocations (when weren't there such periods?!). He wisely disguised his warning to his fellow Jews about the dangers of close relations with the gentiles by this oblique reference to "the many *midrashim* on this section."

V. Rashi Rejects a *Midrash*

While Rashi often makes use of a *midrash* for his purposes, he is by no means bound to accept the *midrash*'s view of a verse. Did he not say "there are many *midrashim* but I have come for the *p'shuto shel mikra*."

Sometimes Rashi will give his interpretation and then add the words like:

ויש מדרשי אגדה... (בראשית ג:כב)

ומדרשי אגדה יש... (בראשית ג:כד)

"and there are *midrashim*..."

In such cases it is obvious that Rashi, while noting the existence of *midrashim* on the verse, nevertheless offers his *p'shat* interpretation as preferable.

What is less obvious are the instances when Rashi offers a simple *p'shat* interpretation, without adding the words "and there are *midrashim*." Occasionally there are comments that are so simple and obvious that it is difficult to understand why Rashi saw the need to make the comment at all. In these cases the super-commentaries struggle to understand Rashi, that is, to understand what prompted him to make the obvious comment.

Following is a striking example of this:

Genesis 48:16

הַמַּלְאָךְ הַגֹּאֵל אֹתִי מִכָּל־רָע יְבָרֵךְ אֶת־הַנְּעָרִים וְיִקָּרֵא בָהֶם שְׁמִי
וְשֵׁם אֲבֹתַי אַבְרָהָם וְיִצְחָק וְיִדְגּוּ לָרֹב בְּקֶרֶב הָאָרֶץ.

יברך את הנערים. מנשה ואפרים.
He shall bless the lads: *Rashi*: Menasseh and Ephraim.

Rashi's comment seems absolutely unnecessary. Anyone reading these verses would never had thought that "the lads" referred to anyone other than Menasseh and Ephraim. Why, then, the need to comment?

The commentaries, *Mizrachi*, *Gur Aryeh* and others spend much time and energy trying to explain why Rashi needs to tell us this obvious interpretation. But their explanations seem forced and don't ring true.

When we check the *midrashim* on this verse we get an understanding of what Rashi is doing.

The *midrash* says:

> "**He shall bless the lads**": This is Joshua and Gideon.

Strange to think that "the lads" standing in front of Jacob were Joshua and Gideon. Joshua was Moses' assistant and successor; he lived several hundred years after Jacob. Gideon was one of the judges of Israel and he lived even after Joshua and much later than Jacob. So what does this *midrash* mean?

But if we think about it, we realize that there are several points which make these two individuals akin to the lads standing in front of Jacob.

   * Joshua is of the tribe of Ephraim. Gideon is of the tribe of Menasseh. The offspring of the lads standing in front of Jacob.

   * Jacob says "The angel that redeems me from all evil..." Both Joshua (see Joshua 5:13) and Gideon (see Judges 6:12ff) were met by angels of G-d to save them!

   * Jacob says " he shall bless the lads..." Joshua was called a lad (Exodus 33:11) and Gideon was called "the youngest of his father's house (Judges 6:15)."

We have three points in common for both of these men, which accurately reflect the words of Jacob. So accepting this *midrash* as a *p'shat* of sorts could be understood. This *midrash* may have been well known in Rashi's time. Rashi, by clarifying that these lads are, in fact, Ephraim and Menasseh, makes it clear that he rejects the *midrash* as not being acceptable as *p'shat.*

VI. RASHI RELATES TO THE TORAH-TEXT; *MIDRASH* RELATES TO ITS IDEAS

In all the examples we have analyzed, we have seen a consistent motif running through them. There is a clear difference between Rashi's use of *midrash* in his Torah commentary and the *midrash*'s own use. My daughter, Elisheva, phrased it succinctly: While the *midrash* uses the text to explain an idea; Rashi uses the *midrash* to explain the text. The truth of this theory is brought home with striking clarity in the following example. I became aware of the significance of this Rashi-comment thanks to my daughter, Shira. It will serve as our last example in this introduction, and it can aptly be called:

אחרון אחרון חביב _____

In the following Rashi-comment we also have a familiar Rashi quote. When we compare it with its *midrashic* source, we see clearly what Rashi is doing and what the *midrash* has done.

See Genesis 33:2

Jacob is going to meet his brother Esau and fears he may be attacked by him. So he arranges his camp in a way that will best protect those dearest to him.

וַיָּשֶׂם אֶת־הַשְּׁפָחוֹת וְאֶת־יַלְדֵיהֶן רִאשֹׁנָה וְאֶת־לֵאָה וִילָדֶיהָ אַחֲרֹנִים וְאֶת־רָחֵל וְאֶת־יוֹסֵף אַחֲרֹנִים.

Rashi: The more behind, the more beloved — אחרון אחרון חביב.

Rashi's comment is brief, but very well known.

As you look at it, can you tell to which of his wives this comment refers? To Rachel, to Leah or to the maidservant-wives ?

Rachel was certainly Jacob's most beloved wife. Reason would dictate that when Rashi says אחרון, אחרון חביב the comment refers to her.

But if you look in a *chumash*, you will certainly be surprised to find that the *dibbur hamaschil* of Rashi's comment is:

וְאֶת־לֵאָה וִילָדֶיהָ אַחֲרֹנִים

That, in itself, is puzzling. Why does Rashi refer to *Leah* as "the very last is most beloved"? And when we check Rashi's *midrashic* source the puzzle is compounded.

In *Bereishis Rabbah*, it says:

> " 'And he put the maidservants and their children first, etc. and Rachel and Joseph last.' This is what is meant: אחרון אחרון חביב ("the more behind, the more beloved")."

Amazing! The *midrash* when it quotes this verse mentions everyone *except* Leah and her children! And Rashi, who quotes this *midrash*, when he quotes the verse mentions *only* Leah and her children!

A true conundrum.

Why did Rashi do this? This is not a printer's error. It is, rather, a striking example of Rashi's work as a Torah commentary and how it differs from the work of the *midrash*.

To understand this we must review what is going on in the Jacob/Esau story. Jacob is coming to meet Esau after 22 years of separation. Jacob fears that Esau will attack him and his family. So in order to protect them as best as he can, he lines them up in reversed order of their importance (love) to him. So that if, G-d forbid, Esau does attack, the least vital will bear the brunt, while hopefully the others will escape. Placing someone first in a dangerous situation isn't very pleasant. This matter of sorting out priorities in a time of crises is known to medical doctors — it is called "triage." Saving a life by sacrificing another is never an easy choice. It is what Jacob was forced to do under the circumstances.

Now, bear in mind that we have two separate objects of analysis:

1) What Jacob did when he was to meet his brother Esau.

2) *What* the Torah says he did and *how* the Torah says it.

This difference between the two is crucial if we are to understand Rashi's use of *midrash*.

The *midrash* is commenting on what Jacob did; his ordering of his wives teaches us the principle of אחרון אחרון חביב. The *midrash* therefore quoted only the first group, the maidservants, and the last group, Rachel and Joseph. By pointing them out, the *midrash* makes its point, for we see the groups are ordered from least to most important. Mentioning Leah was not necessary to make this point.

Rashi, on the other hand, was interpreting *what* the Torah said and *how* it said it. The Torah said:

$$\text{וְאֶת־לֵאָה וִילָדֶיהָ אַחֲרֹנִים}$$

"Leah and her children, **last**."

But Leah was not "last," Rachel was last! Why does the Torah say Leah was "last"? This is what was bothering Rashi and this is what he commented on. He used the *midrash* to explain the meaning of the Torah's word אחרונים. It now means "later," not "last" "Leah and her children *later*." On these words Rashi makes his comment which comes from the *midrash*: "The later (in line), the more beloved." And that is why the expression is not merely אחרון חביב which would mean "the last is the most beloved." It is rather אחרון אחרון חביב which means that the later in line is more beloved than the one before it. So Leah is more beloved than the maidservants, and that is the significance of the word אחרונים. Nevertheless since she comes before Rachel she is not as beloved as Rachel.

That is what Rashi is teaching us. We now understand that the word אחרונים in reference to Leah *is* appropriate; for while she is not last, she is, nevertheless, later than the maidservants and more beloved than they were. It is important to grasp that Rashi is concerned with *how the Torah expressed* the order of Jacob's entourage more than he is concerned about the actual arrangement itself.

The Central Lesson

Rashi and the *midrash* have different goals in commentary. The particular comparison of Rashi and the *midrash* we just discussed places this difference in bold relief. As we noted, Rashi comments on the Torah's words; the *midrash* comments on the Torah's ideas. Keeping this in mind, we can understand why Rashi selects one *midrash* over another; why he will change the location of a *midrash*; change the wording of a *midrash*; or why he may reject a *midrash* altogether.

Rashi's Introduction to Sefer Vayikra

Without formality or fanfare Rashi's opening comment reveals the relationship between G-d's word and His love for His people.

Leviticus 1:1

וַיִּקְרָא אֶל־מֹשֶׁה וַיְדַבֵּר הי אֵלָיו מֵאֹהֶל מוֹעֵד לֵאמֹר.

וַיִּקְרָא אֶל מֹשֶׁה. לכל דברות ולכל אמירות ולכל צווים קדמה קריאה, לשון חיבה לשון שמלאכי השרת משתשמין בו שנאמר וקרא זה אל זה ואמר (ישי ו') אבל לנביאי אומות העולם נגלה עליהן בלשון עראי וטמאה שנאמר ויקר אלוקים אל בלעם (במי כ"ג).

And He called to Moses: *Rashi*: For all "speakings" and all "sayings" and all "commands," a calling preceded them; an expression of endearment, an expression which the ministering angels use, as it says "and one called to the other and said", "ויקרא זה אל זה ואמר" (Isaiah 6:3). But to the prophets of the nations of the world He revealed Himself with a term of happenstance and impurity as it says "G-d happened (ויקר) upon Bilaam" (Numbers 23:4).

Rashi's Opening Comments _____

While this is a very complex comment as we shall see, nevertheless its basic message is clear: *Hashem* has a special love for His People, Israel, and for their prophets. In this introductory comment to the book of Leviticus, we see a recurring theme in Rashi's Torah commentary, i.e., the emphasis on G-d's love for His people. Notice Rashi's consistency in this matter. His first comment on each and every one of the Five Books of the Torah carries this theme. Let's see.

Genesis 1:1

...ומה טעם פתח בבראשית משום כח מעשיו הגיד לעמו לתת
להם נחלת גוים (תהילים קי"א:ו) שאם יאמרו אומות העולם

לישראל ליסטים אתם שכבשתם ארצות שבעה גוים **הם אומרים**
להם כל הארץ של הקב"ה היא הוא בראה ונתנה לאשר ישר
בעיניו ברצונו נתנה להם וברצונו נטלה מהם ונתנה לנו.
...They (Israel) will say to them "The whole earth belongs to the Holy One, blessed be He. He created it, and
He gave it to the one **who was right in His eyes**, He
willingly gave it to them and He willingly took it from
them and gave it to us."

Exodus 1:1

אע"פ שמנאן בחייהם בשמותם חזר ומנאם במיתתם **להודיע**
חיבתם שנמשלו לכוכבים שמוציאן ומכניסן במספר ובשמותם.
...to make known how dear they were [to Him]...

Numbers 1:1

מתוך חיבתן לפניו מונה אותם כל שעה. כשיצאו ממצרים מנאן
וכשנפלו בעגל מנאן לידע הנותרים וכשבא להשרות שכינתו
עליהם מנאם, וכו'.
**Because they were dear to Him, He counted them fre-
quently.**

Deuteronomy 1:1

לפי שהן דברי תוכחות ומנה כאן כל המקומות שהכעיסו לפני
המקום בהן **לפיכך סתם את הדברים והזכירן ברמז מפני כבודן**
של ישראל.
**Therefore He said these words (of reproof) in an ob-
scure manner and mentioned them only with hints,
due to the honor of Israel.**

RASHI AND *MIDRASH*

Note that Rashi selects and emphasizes the word "en*dear*ment" in our
verse and in two other verses. When he doesn't use that term he uses
other words of praise like "honor of Israel" and "to whom it was right in
His eyes."

Certainly this is no coincidence. It is Rashi's way of inspiring the student and making him aware of Israel's special place in G-d's scheme.
Considering the Jews' downtrodden position in the world at the time
when Rashi wrote his commentary (late 11th century), when the Jews
were subject to the cruelties of the Crusades, we can understand Rashi's

desire to lift their spirits and make them aware of their special task in this world.

An Ancient Tradition

But, in truth, the relationship between G-d's love for His people and the study of His word (the Torah) has an ancient tradition. The concept is centrally located in our daily prayers. The prayer said before we recite the *Shema*, morning and evening, is for the study of Torah. That prayer, אהבה רבה, not coincidentally, begins and ends with the word אהבה. *Hashem*'s love literally surrounds the study of Torah. This too is Rashi's message to us as we begin the study of the Book of Leviticus. We see not only G-d's love and compassion for Israel, we see, as well, Rashi's love for his fellow Jews.

❖❖❖

פרשת ויקרא

Rashi stitches together several midrashim to compose his opening comment to the Book of Leviticus, highlighting meaningful nuances in the text.

Leviticus 1:1

וַיִּקְרָא אֶל־מֹשֶׁה וַיְדַבֵּר הי אֵלָיו מֵאֹהֶל מוֹעֵד לֵאמֹר.

ויקרא אל משה. לכל דברות ולכל אמירות ולכל צווים קדמה קריאה, לשון חיבה לשון שמלאכי השרת משתשמין בו שנאמר וקרא זה אל זה ואמר (ישי' ו') אבל לנביאי אומות העולם נגלה עליהן בלשון עראי וטומאה שנאמר ויקר אלוקים אל בלעם (במ' כ"ג).

And He called to Moses: *Rashi:* For all "speakings" and all "sayings" and all "commands," a calling preceded them; an expression of endearment, an expression which the ministering angels use, as it says "and one called to the other and said", "ויקרא זה אל זה ואמר" (Isaiah 6:3). But to the prophets of the nations of the world He revealed Himself with a term of happenstance and impurity as it says "G-d happened (ויקר) upon Bilaam" (Numbers 23:4).

What Is Rashi Saying?

This is a relatively long comment for Rashi. In it he informs us of several things:

1. That whenever the Torah says that G-d spoke to Moses, that communication was preceded by a "calling" even though the Torah does not usually record that "calling."

2. That this "calling" is a sign of endearment.

3. That this sign was unique to the prophets of Israel.

Rashi derives all of this from the words of the Torah. What would you ask?

YOUR QUESTION:

QUESTIONING RASHI

A Question: How does this verse lead one to Rashi's conclusions?

What's bothering Rashi here?

Look carefully at the whole verse.

YOUR ANSWER:

WHAT IS BOTHERING RASHI?

An Answer: A difficulty in this verse is the repetitive use of terms for calling, i.e., "He called....He said..." In actuality this repetitious style is not unusual in the Tanach. But in other cases when the word ויקרא is followed by the words "he said" or "he spoke" it has one of two meanings. Either it means "to summon," as in Genesis 12:18 "And Pharaoh called (summoned) Abram and he said to him..." Or it means that the calling was directed to a particular person, as in Genesis 3:9 "And *Hashem* G-d called out to Adam (and not to Eve) and He said etc." But neither of these situations exists in our verse. Moses was already in the Tent of Meeting when G-d spoke to him, so there was no need for G-d to "summon" him. And since he was alone in the Tent, G-d did not have to direct His speech to him exclusively. Thus, Rashi is implicitly asking: Why this redundant "calling"?

How does his comment deal with this?

YOUR ANSWER:

UNDERSTANDING RASHI

An Answer: Rashi informs us that the word ויקרא has a third meaning. It can also mean to call someone by their name. So when our verse says "He called to Moses" it really means "He called out 'Moses.' " Rashi further informs us, that calling someone by their name is a sign of love. This can be attested to by our own experience. When we speak to someone, we make our conversation more intimate when we refer to our fellow conversationalist by his own name (as any insurance salesman knows!). Likewise here, when *Hashem* called to Moses in the Tent of Meeting, He first addressed him by his name: 'Moses.'

But Rashi says more than this. He says that the words ויקרא אליו express more than merely a personalized communication; they express endearment. What does he mean?

To understand Rashi here we should refer back to the first time *Hashem* spoke to Moses. In Exodus 3:4 we find the following:

וַיַּרְא הי' כִּי סָר לִרְאוֹת וַיִּקְרָא אֵלָיו אֱלֹקִים מִתּוֹךְ הַסְּנֶה וַיֹּאמֶר
מֹשֶׁה מֹשֶׁה וַיֹּאמֶר הִנֵּנִי.

And He saw that he turned aside to see and **G-d called to him** from the midst of the bush and **He said 'Moses, Moses'** and he said 'Here am I.'

Note: Here we have practically the same formula "He (G-d) called to him.....and He said...." But here it says explicitly that G-d called Moses' name. In fact, He called Moses' name twice! This is the sign of endearment that Rashi is referring to.

Calling a person's name twice shows an affection for the person. As is known, enemies refrain from even mentioning their antagonist's name. Contrariwise, calling your friend's name not once but twice reinforces the feeling of closeness to him. Likewise we find G-d calling to Abraham twice (Genesis 22:11), and to Jacob twice (Genesis 46:2). David's haunting lament when he learns of his son Absalom's death, is a chilling reminder of how strong emotions evoke a repetition of a loved one's name.

My son Absalom, my son, my son, Absalom! (Samuel II 19:1).

THE MINISTERING ANGELS

Rashi strengthens his statement by citing the case of the ministering angels. The complete quote from Isaiah (ch. 6) comes from the description of Isaiah's mystical vision of *Hashem* sitting on His Heavenly Throne with the *seraphim* (angels) surrounding Him.

"And one **called** to another and **said** 'Holy, holy, holy is *Hashem*, the Master of legions; the whole world is filled with His glory.'"

Here we have the exact same formula: One *called* and then he *said*. We see that the angels also "*call* to one another" before they "*say*" something.

But we could ask: Where does this verse hint at them calling out by name?

A difficult question. Can you suggest an answer?

YOUR ANSWER:

An Answer: The Radak, Rav Dovid Kimchi, a classical Tanach commentator, suggests the following interpretation. He says that every angel's name is "Holy."

Thus when they say "Holy, holy, holy..." this means that each angel calls a fellow angel by his name twice ("Holy, Holy") and then says to him "holy is *Hashem*." Now we read that verse this way: "And one called to another 'Holy, Holy'...holy is *Hashem*..." This is an original interpretation and accords with what Rashi is telling us. The ministering angel called his fellow angel with affection, by pronouncing his name twice before he began his communication to him.

A CLOSER LOOK _____

וַיִּקְרָא אֶל־מֹשֶׁה...וַיִּקְרָא לְמֹשֶׁה.

Let us take a closer look at the words of the Torah. The Hebrew words ויקרא אל משה (or ויקרא אליו) do not have the same meaning as the words ויקרא למשה.

Unfortunately both are translated in English as "And He called to Moses" but they are not identical. What is the difference between them? Let us look at some examples to see.

וַיִּקְרָא אֲבִימֶלֶךְ לְאַבְרָהָם וַיֹּאמֶר לוֹ... (בראשית כ:ט)
And Abimelech called to Abraham and said to him...

וַיִּקְרָא לְמֹשֶׁה וּלְאַהֲרֹן לַיְלָה וַיֹּאמֶר... (שמות יב:לא)
And he called to Moses and to Aaron at night and he said...

וַיֵּרֶד הי עַל־הַר סִינַי...וַיִּקְרָא הי לְמֹשֶׁה אֶל־רֹאשׁ הָהָר... (שמות יט:כ)
And *Hashem* descended upon Mount Sinai...and *Hashem* called Moses to the top of the mountain...

Compare these verses with the following:

וַיִּקְרָא הי אֱלֹקִים אֶל־הָאָדָם וַיֹּאמֶר לוֹ אַיֶּכָּה. (בראשית ג:ט)
And *Hashem*, G-d, called to the Man and He said to him 'Where are you?'

וַיִּקְרָא אֵלָיו מַלְאַךְ הי מִן הַשָּׁמַיִם וַיֹּאמֶר אַבְרָהָם אַבְרָהָם...
(בראשית כב:יא)

And an angel of *Hashem* called to him from the heavens
and he said 'Abraham, Abraham'...

Do you see a difference between these two groups? What is it?

YOUR ANSWER:

A Significant Difference

An Answer: In the first group, it seems to be saying that, for example, Abimelech
summoned Abraham to come to him; only after Abraham had come
to him did Abimelech say to him whatever he said. Likewise, Pharaoh summoned Moses and Aaron to come to him. And, in our
third example, *Hashem* summoned Moses to come to the top of the
mountain.

In the second group, there was no summoning. *Hashem* says to
Adam, "Where are you?" G-d is not summoning him, He is calling
out to him. The angel is not summoning Abraham. Nor is it likely
that ויקרא means "calls his attention" in these verses. A voice from
heaven is startling enough, one needn't be called to attention to
listen to it. If these words don't mean "to summon", what do they
mean?

The *Havanas Hamikra* offers a brilliant insight. He says that whenever
it says ויקרא אל it means that the person was called by his name. So if it
says in our verse ויקרא אל משה וידבר ה' אליו (and not ויקרא למשה), it
means that G-d called Moses *by his name*.

This subtle difference in language between these nearly identical phrases
is an example of the nuances of language which one finds in biblical
Hebrew. Rashi was aware of this nuance. It forms the basis for his comment here.

There is a passage in the Tanach which gives unequivocal support that
the words ויקרא אל mean to call by name. Can you find it? You must be
familiar with Tanach, the Book of Samuel to be precise, in order to remember it.

YOUR ANSWER:

THE PROOFTEXT

An Answer: When the young prophet Samuel received his very first prophetic vision, he was inexperienced with prophecy so that initially he didn't know he was experiencing a communication from G-d. Look closely at this passage from I Samuel 3:4-10.

> "And *Hashem* called to Samuel (ויקרא ה' אל שמואל) and he said 'Here I am.' He ran to Eli and said 'Here I am, for you called me.' But he said 'I did not call; go back and lie down.' *Hashem* continued to call again 'Samuel!' so Samuel rose and went to Eli and said 'Here I am, for you called me.' But he said 'I did not call you, my son, go back and lie down.' Samuel had not yet known *Hashem* and the word of *Hashem* had not yet been revealed to him. *Hashem* continued to call, 'Samuel' a third time and he arose and went to Eli and said, 'Here I am, for you called me.' Then Eli realized that *Hashem* was calling the lad. Eli said to Samuel 'Go lie down and if He calls you, you should say 'Speak, *Hashem*, for Your servant is listening.' Samuel went and lay down in the place. *Hashem* came and appeared and called as the other times , 'Samuel, Samuel' and Samuel said 'Speak for Your servant is listening.' "

This is a convincing example that the words ויקרא אל mean that someone was addressed by their name.

* First of all, the passage begins with these words: ויקרא ה' אל שמואל and not ויקרא לשמואל.

* Secondly, Samuel's name must have been called, otherwise he wouldn't have run to Eli thinking that Eli had called him.

* Thirdly, it says explicitly that G-d called "as the other times 'Samuel, Samuel'..."

Here we have the double name, which is the sign of endearment that Rashi referred to.

In SUMMARY

We see how Rashi finds meaningful messages even from the slightest verbal variations. As a consequence we learn to appreciate the fine distinctions in biblical Hebrew.

(See *Havanas Hamikra*)

Rashi and Ramban disagree over simple p'shat.

Leviticus 2:14

וְאִם־תַּקְרִיב מִנְחַת בִּכּוּרִים לַֽיהֹוָ֑ה אָבִ֞יב קָל֤וּי בָּאֵשׁ֙ גֶּ֣רֶשׂ כַּרְמֶ֔ל תַּקְרִ֕יב
אֵ֖ת מִנְחַ֥ת בִּכּוּרֶֽיךָ.

וְאִם תַּקְרִיב. הֲרֵי ׳אִם׳ מְשַׁמֵּשׁ בִּלְשׁוֹן ׳כִּי׳ שֶׁהֲרֵי אֵין זֶה רְשׁוּת
שֶׁהֲרֵי בְּמִנְחַת הָעֹמֶר הַכָּתוּב מְדַבֵּר שֶׁהִיא חוֹבָה וְכֵן וְאִם יִהְיֶה
הַיּוֹבֵל וְגוֹ׳ (במ׳ ל״ו:ד).

And if you offer: *Rashi*: The word אם here has the meaning of כי "when", (and not its usual meaning of "if") for
this (offering of the firstfruits) is not optional since Scripture is speaking of the meal-offering of the *Omer* which
is obligatory. Likewise (the word אם in) וְאִם יִהְיֶה הַיּוֹבֵל
which means "when the Jubilee will come" (and not "*If
the Jubilee will come.*")

WHAT IS RASHI SAYING?

Rashi is clarifying a very simple point. The word אם, which usually
means "if", cannot mean that here, since the *Omer* offering (which is the
subject of this verse) is obligatory and must be brought. Instead the word
אם is to be translated as "when" a meaning it sometimes carries.

A DEEPER LOOK

This seems very obvious and straightforward. Yet the Ramban offers a
p'shat explanation that allows us to leave the word אם meaning "if."
Read through all the verses from the beginning of chapter 2. Pay special
attention to these verses: 2:1, 2:4, 2:5, 2:7, and our verse 2:14.

Can you offer an explanation which has the word אם meaning "if" even
though the verse refers to the obligatory offering of the *Omer*? Can you
figure out the Ramban's interpretation?

YOUR ANSWER:

THE RAMBAN'S P'SHAT INTERPRETATION

The Ramban points out that our chapter begins with a general heading
(2:1): "When a soul will offer a meal offering to *Hashem*, of fine flour

should be his offering etc." Then the Torah goes on to enumerate the various types of meal-offerings, one of them being the *Omer* offering. Thus, the Ramban says, it is as if the Torah is saying: "When you offer a meal-offering do it this way. *If* it is one that is prepared in a pan (2:5), or *if* it is one that is prepared in a boiling pot (2:7), or *if* you offer a meal-offering of first grains etc." (2:14)

Looked at in this way, the "אם" here means: "If" the meal-offering which is brought is the *Omer* offering, then etc. It does not mean "If" he will bring the *Omer* offering.

In short, the Ramban is saying that one needn't change the meaning of אם to "when" as Rashi does. Its meaning can remain "if" and still make perfect sense in the context.

Defending Rashi

Can you defend Rashi against the Ramban's interpretation? Can you think why Rashi nevertheless saw the need to change the meaning of אם from "if" to "when" ?

Hint: Compare verses 2:5 and 2:7 with our verse. Do you see any difference between them?

Your Answer:

A Closer Look

An Answer: Let us look closely at those verses.

Leviticus 2:5

וְאִם־מִנְחָה עַל הַמַּחֲבַת קָרְבָּנֶךָ וגו'

If meal (baked) in a frying pan is your offering etc.

Leviticus 2:7

וְאִם־מִנְחַת מַרְחֶשֶׁת קָרְבָּנֶךָ וגו'

If meal (prepared) in a boiling pot is your offering etc.

Our Verse:

וְאִם־תַּקְרִיב מִנְחַת בִּכּוּרִים לַה'

If you offer an oblation of first fruits etc.

Do you notice any difference between the first two verses and our verse?

YOUR ANSWER:

An Answer: The first two verses place the word "אם" before the type of offering, as if to give us the various possibilities of meal offerings that
exist, as the Ramban explained. But our verse places the "אם" before the words "you offer," as if there were a choice between offering or not offering the first fruits! It is for this reason that Rashi did
not accept the Ramban's explanation of our verse. He thus saw the
need to change the meaning of the word אם from "if" to "when" in
this verse.

Lesson

The Ramban's *p'shat* interpretations throughout the Torah are very reasonable and convincing. But Rashi should never be dispensed with, out
of hand. A close look at the Torah's words frequently reveals a subtle
basis for his interpretation.

(See *Ramban*)

Leviticus 4:3

אִם הַכֹּהֵן הַמָּשִׁיחַ יֶחֱטָא לְאַשְׁמַת הָעָם וְהִקְרִיב עַל חַטָּאתוֹ אֲשֶׁר חָטָא פַּר בֶּן־בָּקָר תָּמִים לַה' לְחַטָּאת.

אם הכהן המשיח יחטא לאשמת העם: מדרשו – אינו חיב אלא בהעלם דבר עם שגגת מעשה, כמו שנאמר לאשמת העם "ונעלם דבר מעיני הקהל ועשו" ופשוטו לפי האגדה – כשכהן גדול חוטא אשמת העם הוא זה, שהן תלוין בו לכפר עליהם ולהתפלל בעדם, ונעשה מקולקל.

If the anointed priest will sin, to the guilt of the people: *Rashi*: The *midrashic* interpretation is — that he is only obligated (to bring an offering) if there was ignorance of the law together with an unintentional deed, as it says in reference to the guilt of the whole people "(And if the whole congregation of Israel sin) and the matter be hid from the eyes of the assembly and they have done...." But its *p'shat* sense is according to the aggadic explanation — When the High Priest sins this is to the guilt of the people (i.e., the people remain under a burden of guilt) because they are dependent on him to effect atonement for them and to pray on their behalf, but now he has become impaired (i.e., incapable of interceding on their behalf).

WHAT IS RASHI SAYING?

This is a complex Rashi with certain halachic assumptions which must be spelled out before we can understand it. Let us first explain it, then we will analyze it.

The laws in this section deal with various situations where someone has sinned unintentionally. The two cases that concern us here are:

1) When the High Priest sins.

2) When the whole assembly sins unintentionally.

The latter case refers to a situation where the Sanhedrin, referred to as "the eyes of the assembly," promulgated a law incorrectly and the people followed their incorrect ruling. In our verse, however, we have no indication what the circumstances were of the High Priest's sinning. A connection is proposed between the High Priest's sin and that of the congregation.

What would you ask on this complex comment?

YOUR QUESTION:

QUESTIONING RASHI _____

A Question: Why the need to compare our verse with the case of the whole
assembly sinning? What is bothering Rashi that he need offer this
interpretation?

YOUR ANSWER:

WHAT IS BOTHERING RASHI? _____

An Answer: The words "to the guilt of the people" are strange here and appear
to be out of place. What has the High Priest's sin got to do with the
"guilt of the people"? It is *his* guilt that is the issue, not the congre-
gations.

It is this difficulty that Rashi's comment addresses.

He offers two answers: one a *midrash* and one *p'shat* according to the
aggadah.

How do these answers clarify matters?

YOUR ANSWER:

UNDERSTANDING RASHI'S *MIDRASH* _____

An Answer: The *drash* is based on the verse's associating the High Priest's sin
with the "guilt of the people." As we noted, the circumstances of
"people sinning" are spelled out in the Torah, while the circumstances the High Priest's sinning are not spelled out. We know from
verse 4:13 of the people's sin. "If the entire congregation shall *err*
and a matter became *obscured from the eyes* of the congregation
(*viz.* the Sanhedrin) and they commit ..." etc. These, then, are the
two conditions in the case of the "guilt of the people." Because of
the "out-of-place" words לאשמת העם in our verse, the *drash* con-
nects the two cases and applies the known laws of the congregation's
sinning (the two conditions mentioned above) to the unknown situation of the High Priest sinning. So we learn that the High Priest is
only obligated to bring a guilt-offering if his sin was also uninten-

tional and done on the basis of an incorrect halachic decision which he made.

In summary, the *drash* part of Rashi's comment uses the words "to the guilt of the people" to make a bridge to the laws of the congregation's sinning and, in so doing, to learn the laws of the High Priest's sinning. Now let us look at what Rashi calls "*p'shat* according to the *aggadah*."

"P'SHAT ACCORDING TO THE AGGADAH"

Rashi says:

> "But its *p'shat* sense is according to the aggadic explanation — When the High Priest sins this is to the guilt of the people (i.e., the people remain under a burden of guilt) because they are dependent on him to effect atonement for them and to pray on their behalf, but now he has become impaired (i.e., incapable of interceding on their behalf)."

This phrase — "*p'shat* according to the *aggadah*" — is a very unusual phrase. What does it mean? *P'shat* and *aggadah* seem to be opposites or, as is fashionable to say today, "*p'shat* according to *aggadah*" is an oxymoron.

But first let us see Rashi's *midrashic* source.

RASHI'S SOURCE

We find the following in the *midrash aggadah*, Vayikra Rabbah:

> "Rav Chiya learned: Since the anointed one (High Priest) atones and the congregation atones, it is best if the High Priest atones first, as it says 'and he shall atone for himself and for the nation' (Leviticus 16:24).

> "Rav Levi said: Unfortunate is the country whose doctor is sick and whose treasurer has only one eye and whose Attorney General is guilty of murder!" (Sounds familiar!!)

THE MEANING OF THE AGGADAH

The message is abundantly clear: The one who is to intercede for us, to ask forgiveness from G-d for our sins (the High Priest), if he sins, he is himself in need of Divine forgiveness! First he must do his own *teshuva* and achieve atonement before he can be the people's emissary to G-d to free them of their guilt.

Now we can make sense out our verse. The High Priest's sin is considered "the guilt of the congregation" because they are left with no one to intercede on their behalf: they are left with their guilt.

This interpretation is based on the idea found in the *aggadah*. But, in spite of the fact that this comes from an *aggadah*, it sounds like a *p'shat* interpretation of the verse. It appeals to our reason and common sense. Yet its source is the *aggadah* in Vayikra Rabbah. This is Rashi's meaning when he says "the *p'shat* is according to the *aggadah*."

RASHI AND *MIDRASH*

We have here an unusual case where Rashi uses the conceptual kernel of a *midrash*, without using its terminology or its analogy. This is what he means by his words "the *P'shat* is according the aggadah." He means to say "according to the *idea of the* aggadah." This has confused some students of Rashi. They could not find any aggadah that said exactly what Rashi says, so they concluded that the aggadah he referred to has been lost. It has not been lost, it has been used by Rashi but in his own words.

❖❖❖

A morally inspiring comment, whose psychological kernel is eternally true.

Leviticus 4: 22

אֲשֶׁר נָשִׂיא יֶחֱטָא וְעָשָׂה אַחַת מִכָּל־מִצְוֹת הי אֱלֹקָיו אֲשֶׁר לֹא־
תֵעָשֶׂינָה בִּשְׁגָגָה וְאָשֵׁם.

אשר נשיא יחטא. לשון אשרי, אשרי הדור שהנשיא שלו נותן
לב להביא כפרה על שגגתו, קל וחומר שמתחרט על זדונותיו.
When a Prince sins: *Rashi*: [אשר] is an expression of
אשרי, "good fortune." Fortunate is the generation whose
leader is concerned to bring an atonement for his inadvertent sins, all the more so would he regret his intentional sins.

WHAT IS RASHI SAYING?

This comment is based on a word-play. The Torah says אשר נשיא יחטא and Rashi finds this similar to the word אשרי which means "happy is" or "fortunate is." From that play on words, it is but a short leap to the moral lesson about the humble, honest prince.

What would you ask here?

YOUR QUESTION:

QUESTIONING RASHI

A Question: Granted the play on words is clever, but why the need for it? Why does Rashi cite this *drash* (it certainly is not *p'shat*)?

What is bothering him?

Hint: Compare our verse with other verses in this *parasha* where the Torah mentions people sinning and their obligation to bring a sacrifice.

YOUR ANSWER:

WHAT IS BOTHERING RASHI?

An Answer: Similar verses appear in our sedra. They are:

אִם הַכֹּהֵן הַמָּשִׁיחַ יֶחֱטָא לְאַשְׁמַת הָעָם וגו' (ויקרא ד:ג)

If the anointed priest should sin to the guilt on the people etc. (Leviticus 4:3)

וְאִם כָּל־עֲדַת יִשְׂרָאֵל יִשְׁגּוּ וְנֶעְלַם דָּבָר מֵעֵינֵי הַקָּהָל וגו' (ד:יג)

If the entire congregation of Israel erred and the matter be hid from eyes of the assembly etc. (Leviticus 4:13)

וְאִם־נֶפֶשׁ אַחַת תֶּחֱטָא בִשְׁגָגָה מֵעַם הָאָרֶץ וגו' (ד:כז)

If a person unwittingly sins, one of the ordinary people, etc. (Leviticus 4:27)

But in our verse we have:

אֲשֶׁר נָשִׂיא יֶחֱטָא וגו'

When a Prince sins etc.

Rashi was sensitive to this deviation from the usual language used in this sedra. Thus he commented on the word אשר, which is unusual.

How does his comment explain this difference?

YOUR ANSWER:

UNDERSTANDING RASHI

An Answer: The use of אשר signified a special message: that the sinning of the Prince, and his recognition and confession of guilt, constitutes a special occasion. The Prince (also refers to a king or a president), being the highest authority in the community, had no one above him to fear. He was the apex of communal power. No one, no power, could enforce the law upon him; no one could punish him for his crimes or misdemeanors. This is a unique situation. The ordinary citizen, even the virtuous one, lives in constant apprehension, albeit unconscious, that if he is caught at a misdeed, he may be personally punished and publicly embarrassed. This has a profound deterrent effect on most people. Not so the Prince. He lives, as it were, above the law. He, being the highest authority, need not fear his underlings prosecuting or punishing him. *He* could dispense with *them*; not *they* with *him*.

So, if we have a Prince who, in spite of his unchallenged power, is willing, of his own volition, to admit his guilt, this is quite unusual and significantly praiseworthy.

This is the point of Rashi's comment. Such an example of confession by a community leader is found in the case of Judah (Genesis 38:26) where he admits to having fathered Tamar's child (children), when he could most easily have escaped detection by remaining silent. But he chose to admit his guilt.

A CLOSER LOOK

Why do you think Rashi says "Happy is the generation" and not simply "Happy is the prince"?

YOUR ANSWER:

An Answer: It would be somewhat inapt to say "Happy is the prince who sins and admits his sin!" Sinning is never a time for rejoicing. The congregation, on the other hand, did not sin. Their good fortune of having an honest, humble leader is untainted by sin.

A DEEPER LOOK

Rashi bases his comment on the word אשר, translating it as "happy." What would he say to the following verse in I Kings 15:30.

עַל־חַטֹּאות יָרָבְעָם אֲשֶׁר חָטָא וַאֲשֶׁר הֶחֱטִיא אֶת־יִשְׂרָאֵל בְּכַעְסוֹ
אֲשֶׁר הִכְעִיס אֵת הי אֱלֹקֵי יִשְׂרָאֵל.

For the sins of Jeroboam who (אשר) had sinned and who
(אשר) caused Israel to sin, with his provocations by which
he angered *Hashem*, G-d of Israel.

Here we have the same word אשר describing a king's sinning (even used
in describing his causing others to sin!). It is used in reference to Israel's
most notorious king, Jeroboam ben Navat! How can we square this with
Rashi's comment here? Would he also say that generation was fortunate
to have as its king Jeroboam?

YOUR ANSWER:

A Deeper Understanding

An Answer: This question was asked by the Sages. Their answer is illuminating regarding the ways of *drash*. They say that the *drash* on the
word אשר is valid in our verse precisely because the word אשר
deviates from the other verses in this section where the word אם is
used, as we pointed out above. So it not just the word אשר which is
the basis for the *drash*; that together with the fact that it is unusual
in the context. And, of course, in our verse we are speaking of a
case where the king admits his sin, something that Jeroboam did
not do. Therefore since the use of the word אשר in reference to
Jeroboam is neither unusual nor do we find that he confessed his
guilt, thus it does not merit the *drash* interpretation of "fortunate is
the generation." Certainly his generation was far from fortunate
that he was their king.

An Eternal Truth

As these lines are being written the impeachment of the president of the
United States is being voted on. The most powerful man in the world is
being humbled, severely criticized and publicly embarrassed, all because
he could not bring himself to admit to lying, all because he could not say
חטאתי. Most experts agree that if he would have admitted to falsifying
his testimony, the public would have been willing to forgive and forget.
But pride, and the illusory power of his position, make such an admis-
sion appear to be an almost superhuman feat. Everyone would breath
easier, everyone would utter a sigh of relief, everyone would feel

"fortunate" if the "Prince" would admit his guilt. Indeed "fortunate is the generation whose leader can admit his guilt." Rashi's lesson was true thousands of years ago, it is no less true today.

(See *Gur Aryeh, Havanas Hamikra*)

You need to think straight to grasp what Rashi is saying.

Leviticus 5:23

וְהָיָה כִּי־יֶחֱטָא וְאָשֵׁם וְהֵשִׁיב אֶת־הַגְּזֵלָה אֲשֶׁר גָּזָל אוֹ אֶת־הָעֹשֶׁק אֲשֶׁר עָשָׁק אוֹ אֶת־הַפִּקָּדוֹן אֲשֶׁר הָפְקַד אִתּוֹ אוֹ אֶת הָאֲבֵדָה אֲשֶׁר מָצָא.

כי יחטא ואשם. כשיכיר בעצמו לשוב בתשובה ובדעתו להתודות,
כי חטא ואשם.

When he will sin and incur guilt. *Rashi*: When he recognizes by himself the need to repent, and has in mind to confess that he sinned and is guilty.

WHAT IS RASHI SAYING? _____

Rashi tells us that this man has recognized his sin and is committed to doing *teshuva*.

In that case he must return the stolen article, plus a fifth of its value, to the victim and also bring a guilt-offering.

YOUR QUESTION:

QUESTIONING RASHI _____

A Question: Why does Rashi say; "he has in mind to confess"? Why does he add this? The verse does not say this. Where is this hinted at in the verse?

What is bothering Rashi here?

YOUR ANSWER:

WHAT IS BOTHERING RASHI ? _____

An Answer: Rashi is dealing with the phrase "and he will sin and be guilty."
This is a strange statement. Every time a person sins he is guilty!
Can a person sin and not be guilty? It is redundant to say "he will
sin" and then add "and he will be guilty."

To clarify the unusual use of the word ואשם in our verse, let us
compare the word ואשם in our verse with the same word when it is
used in previous verses in this chapter.

אוֹ נֶפֶשׁ אֲשֶׁר תִּגַּע בְּכָל־דָּבָר טָמֵא אוֹ בְנִבְלַת חַיָּה טְמֵאָה אוֹ בְּנִבְלַת
בְּהֵמָה טְמֵאָה אוֹ בְּנִבְלַת שֶׁרֶץ טָמֵא וְנֶעְלַם מִמֶּנּוּ וְהוּא טָמֵא וְאָשֵׁם.
(ויקרא ה:ב)

Or if a person will have touched any impure object...and
he is **impure and became guilty**. (5:2)

אוֹ נֶפֶשׁ כִּי תִשָּׁבַע לְבַטֵּא בִשְׂפָתַיִם לְהָרַע אוֹ לְהֵיטִיב לְכֹל אֲשֶׁר
יְבַטֵּא הָאָדָם בִּשְׁבֻעָה וְנֶעְלַם מִמֶּנּוּ וְהוּא־יָדַע וְאָשֵׁם לְאַחַת מֵאֵלֶּה.
(שם ה:ד)

Or if a person will swear...**and then he knew and he
became guilty** regarding one of these matters. (5:4)

What does the word ואשם mean in these verses?

Hint: See Rashi's comment on this word in verse 5:2. There he says
"after this impurity he eats holy food or enters the Temple." Why does
Rashi add this?

YOUR ANSWER:

UNDERSTANDING RASHI'S DIFFICULTY _____

An Answer: The word ואשם in these verses means to do a sin. In the first verse,
Rashi tells us that the person, after becoming impure, enters the
Temple. This is a sin. While becoming impure is, in itself, no sin,
entering the Temple in an impure state is a sin. Thus the word ואשם
here means that after he became impure he did another act, which
is not mentioned in the verse, he ate holy food or he entered the
Temple — and he is, therefore, guilty.

The second verse tells us of a person who made a vow ואשם and
was guilty. This means that he became guilty by transgressing his
oath (a point not mentioned in the verse). Making a vow, in itself,

is no sin, transgressing it, is. So in each of these verses the word ואשם refers to a separate act which is not mentioned in the verse.

But in our verse ואשם does not seem to have the meaning that the person did some additional act besides stealing. What, then, does the word ואשם mean here?

This is what's bothering Rashi.

How does his comment deal with this?

YOUR ANSWER:

UNDERSTANDING RASHI

An Answer: Rashi tells us that the word ואשם does not have its usual meaning "to be guilty" of a separate act. Our verse is talking about a person who stole something, the act of stealing itself is a sin, as opposed to the cases above, of being impure or making a vow. He tell us that the thief's decision to return the stolen object, indicates he has done *teshuva*. Here, therefore, the word ואשם means, not "he is guilty" but "he recognizes his guilt." The separate "act" is the recognition of his sin and his desire to do *teshuva*.

In summary: The word ואשם here does not mean to *become* guilty, since the man was guilty the moment he stole; it means rather he *recognized his guilt* to the extent that he wants to mend his ways and return the stolen object. Now the verse makes sense and this is precisely what Rashi is telling us: "when he will sin and *recognize his guilt* ..."

(See *Gur Aryeh*)

A puzzling comment, and one that can give us a clue to interpreting puzzling Rashi comments.

Leviticus 5:24

אוֹ מִכֹּל אֲשֶׁר־יִשָּׁבַע עָלָיו לַשֶּׁקֶר וְשִׁלַּם אֹתוֹ בְּרֹאשׁוֹ וַחֲמִשִׁתָיו יֹסֵף עָלָיו לַאֲשֶׁר הוּא לוֹ יִתְּנֶנּוּ בְּיוֹם אַשְׁמָתוֹ.

לַאֲשֶׁר הוּא לוֹ. לְמִי שֶׁהַמָּמוֹן שֶׁלּוֹ.

To whom it belongs: *Rashi*: To whom the money belongs.

A brief comment whose purpose is unclear and which has elicited many interpretations.

What would you ask?

YOUR QUESTION:

QUESTIONING RASHI: _____

A Question: What is Rashi adding that we didn't know before? Of course he returns the money to its owner! That is what the verse says and that is what logic would dictate.

What's bothering Rashi that he needed to make this obvious comment?

YOUR ANSWER:

WHAT IS BOTHERING RASHI ? _____

Some Suggested Answers:

Several different answers have been suggested by the super-commentaries. Let us look at some of them and then see how we can best understand Rashi.

1. "The word 'it' of 'he shall give it' refers to the fifth. 'It' of 'to the one to whom it belongs' might also have been understood as referring to the fifth. But then the verse would be instructing us to give the fifth to the one to whom the fifth belongs without telling us who that is. Rashi therefore explains that 'to the one to whom it belongs' refers to the principal. "

(*Artscroll* citing *Gur Aryeh*)

This is quite complex reasoning and not easy to follow. This is not characteristic of Rashi's style which is usually based on simple and straighforward reasoning. It also assumes that I might have thought that the money should go to someone else (unnamed) besides the victim. Why would I ever think that?

2. Another answer given: "He cannot salve his conscience by donating the sum to charity or the like but he must return it to the man he defrauded."

(The Metsudah Rashi)

This answer is no less difficult to accept. Who would ever think that a person can acquit himself of robbery by giving the stolen money to charity?! Stealing from the rich to give to the poor is fine for Robin Hood, but not for Judaism! Has not the prophet Isaiah (61:8) stated emphatically that G-d "hates robbery in sacrifices."

3. And yet another suggested answer: "He should not give it to a friend or to a relative [of the victim]. This law is not as we find in Numbers 5:10 where it says 'a man's sacred objects shall be his...' From which we derive that the Israelite, who is obligated to give his tithing to a priest, can choose which priest to give it to. Here, however, the verse tells us that he must give the stolen money back to its owner."

(Mizarchi)

This is a strange comparison between the Israelite who is obligated to give a tithing but may choose the priest and the robber who is obligated to return the theft to the victim. The Israelite is giving his tithing to a priest, so the Torah allows him to choose his priest. But in our case, the thief is giving back the owner's own money. He certainly cannot choose to give it to someone else.

So we must search elsewhere for an answer.

A More Basic Question

To understand this we must ask a more basic question: Why does the Torah itself (not just Rashi) tell us the obvious — that he must "give it to whom it belongs"? To whom else would he return it? So the question we asked of Rashi is an equally valid question to ask on the Torah verse. Answering this question will help us understand Rashi.

The Torah must have used these words, emphasizing the obvious, to steer us away from a possible misunderstanding. In our efforts to understand Rashi we should arrive at a better understand of the Torah's meaning of these words.

A Rule in Understanding Rashi

When confronted by such a puzzling comment it is wise to see Rashi's source. (Rashi's sources can be found in Chavel's Rashi or any English translation of Rashi, Artscroll, Silbermann or Metsudah, for example.) In this case, Rashi's source can be found both in the mishnah and in the *midrash Toras Cohanim*.

Let us see what mishnah 9:5 in *Baba Kamma* says (also on page 103a of tractate *Baba Kamma*).

> "If a man steals from his neighbor even a *prutah*'s worth and swears (his innocence) to him, (and then admits his guilt) he must take the money even to Medes (a distant land). *He shall not give it to his son or to his messenger...*"

This last phrase is our clue. "He shall not give it [even] to his son," but rather to the victim himself. In his commentary to the Talmud, Rashi explains that this law derives from our verse "he shall give it to whom it belongs." So we see clearly that Rashi understood the halachic message of this verse to mean that the thief must return the stolen money to the victim and not even to his son. Now we can understand why the Torah stresses the obvious, i.e. that the money must be returned to the victim himself, because it cannot be returned even to his son, which common sense would have thought would be sufficient.

(See *HaKsav V'Hakabalah*)

But we must understand this law. Why cannot the stolen article be returned to the man's son or to a messenger?

Can you think of an explantion?

Your Answer:

A Deeper Look

An Answer: We must bear in mind that this law of stealing (or keeping an object given as a safekeeping) refers to a particular condition: that the man took an oath denying guilt, and only later did he confess.

The Rambam (Laws of Stealing ch. 7:9) offers an explanation for the requirement to return the theft personally to the victim and not through a messenger. He says that once the thief swore that he did not take the stolen goods, the victim gave up all hope of ever retrieving it. He saw the robber swear under oath in a court of law, which is certainly no less an awesome experience than taking a lie detector test, and nevertheless he denied all guilt. Seeing this, the victim's last thread of hope vanished, thinking that now he would never get his money back. Therefore, says the Rambam, the thief must make a special effort to return it to the man personally, to be 100% sure he receives it. Perhaps in order to shorten as much as possible the latter's distress.

I would suggest another possible answer to the question as to why the Torah stresses that the thief must personally return the money to the victim.

We see that the fact that he swore falsely is the crucial ingredient in this case. As it says at the beginning of this chapter: (5:21)

> "If a person will sin and commit a trespass against *Hashem* and be deceitful toward his friend regarding a pledge or about a putting of a hand or about robbery; or deprived his comrade. or he found a lost item and denied it - and he swore falsely about any of all the things, which man does do, to sin by them — so it shall be that he will sin and become guilty, he will return the robbed item that he robbed or the proceeds of his fraud or the pledge that was left with him or the lost item that he found, or anything about which he had sworn falsely — he shall repay its capital and its fifths; he shall give it to the one to whom it belongs on the day he admits his guilt. And he shall bring his guilt-offering to *Hashem* — an unblemished ram from the flock, of the value for a guilt-offering — to the priest."

His false oath has caused him to pay the additional fifth and to bring a guilt-offering. The guilt-offering is atonement for the false oath which is a sin against G-d. Now notice an unusual phrase in this verse.

> "...he shall give it to whom it belongs *on the day of his guilt-offering** (ביום אשמתו)"

What is the point of these latter words? Why is the day of his guilt-offering stressed? Why can't he bring his guilt-offering and then, on the next day, "he shall give it to whom it belongs"?

An explanation may be: The law is that one *may not* bring a sin-offering before he has returned the money (Tractate *Baba Kamma* 110a). Only

---

* The correct translation of the words ביום אשמתו are by no means agreed upon. Most translations have "on the day of his guilt" or "on the day he acknowledges his guilt." But the Metsuda Chumash has "on the day of his guilt-offering." The source of this interpretation is the *Chizkuni*, an early Torah commentator. I have chosen this translation because it helps us understand the reason for his having to return the stolen article directly to the owner.

after returning the money, is the Temple offering valid. This coincides with the general laws of repentance. Man must first be forgiven by his fellowman, before G-d will forgive him. This, then, may be the reason why the Torah emphasizes that a man must return *to the owner* the money and not rely on someone else — a son or messenger — to do it. He must be certain that he has made full amends *before* ("on the day of his guilt offering", ביום אשמתו) he is allowed to bring his offering.

An Important Lesson in Rashi

An important lesson can be learned from the above analysis. As we have explained (see "Appreciating Rashi" in the *Bereishis* volume), one of the basic types of Rashi-comments is what I have called the Type II comment. This is the short comment whose purpose is to help us avoid a likely misunderstanding. The above Rashi-comment is of this kind. In such cases we don't ask "What is bothering Rashi?" because there is no real difficulty in the verse. We ask, instead, "What misunderstanding is Rashi helping us avoid?" In such cases, it is important to keep in mind that the to-be-avoided interpretation should be truly a reasonable misinterpretation and not some far-out possibility that would rarely occur to anyone.

As we saw with some of the suggested answers above, it is hard to imagine that any student would think, for example, that the stolen money could be given to charity or to anyone whom the thief chooses. It hard to conceive that Rashi saw the need to make his comment in order to reject such unreasonable possibilities. The answer which comes from the Talmud (Rashi's source) *is* a likely misunderstanding, to think that the thief could fulfill his obligation by returning the money to the son of the victim; or to give it to him to pass on to this father, is a most reasonable way of paying back the victim. Therefore Rashi had to clarify that in this particular case (once the thief had sworn falsely) it is not sufficient to repay the debt in this way.

In any Rashi-comment of the Type II kind when trying to understand what interpretation Rashi was rejecting, reasonableness must be our guide. We have not fully understood Rashi by coming up with just *any* possible misinterpretation; we must find a *likely* one. Only then can we be confident that it was this misinterpretation that Rashi is implicitly warning us about. Rashi's thinking is always straightforward, clear and eminently reasonable. Ours must be likewise, in order to understand him.

A straightforward comment whose meaning is less than obvious.

Leviticus 6:2

צַו אֶת־אַהֲרֹן וְאֶת־בָּנָיו לֵאמֹר זֹאת תּוֹרַת הָעֹלָה הִוא הָעֹלָה עַל
מוֹקְדָה עַל־הַמִּזְבֵּחַ כָּל־הַלַּיְלָה עַד־הַבֹּקֶר וְאֵשׁ הַמִּזְבֵּחַ תּוּקַד בּוֹ.

צַו אֶת אהרן. אֵין צַו אֶלָּא לְשׁוֹן זֵרוּז מִיָּד וּלְדוֹרוֹת. אָמַר רַבִּי
שִׁמְעוֹן, בְּיוֹתֵר צָרִיךְ הַכָּתוּב לְזָרֵז בְּמָקוֹם שֶׁיֵּשׁ בּוֹ חֶסְרוֹן כִּיס.
Command Aaron: *Rashi:* The word צו is an expression
of "urging" both immediately and for future generations. Said Rabbi Shimon: It is especially necessary for
the Scriptures to urge [this commandment] in a case where
monetary loss is involved.

RASHI'S SOURCE

Rashi's source is the *midrash halacha, Toras Cohanim* (also the Talmud
Kedushin 29b). There is a somewhat complex derivation based on a comparison with other verses where the word צו or מצוה is used. The literal
meaning of the word צו is "command." But the added meaning of "urging" is derived from a verse in Deuteronomy 3:28. "But you should
command Joshua and strengthen him and give him resolve..." This verse
conveys the sense of זירוז of urging Joshua to do his task well. The idea
of "immediately and for future generations" is derived from a verse in
Numbers 15:23. "Everything that *Hashem* has *commanded* you through
Moses from the day that *Hashem commanded* and onward throughout
your generations."

This is the *midrashic* derivation of Rashi's comment.

Have you got a question on his comment?

YOUR QUESTION:

Questioning Rashi

A Question: Why does Rashi have to mention the *midrash* at all?

What is bothering him?

Hint: Compare our verse with Leviticus 1:1,2.

YOUR ANSWER:

What Is Bothering Rashi?

An Answer: The use of the word צו is a departure from the general language used in the Torah when a *mitzvah* is given. For example, the book of Leviticus begins the laws of sacrifices with (1:2) *"Speak* to the children of Israel and *say* to them..."* Most commandments, too numerous to cite, are introduced in this way.

Why the departure from this formula, by using the word צו ?

This may be the spur to Rashi's comment here.

How does Rashi (and the *midrash*) help us understand the verse?

YOUR ANSWER:

Understanding Rashi

Rashi felt the need to comment here and use the *midrash* to explain the loaded meaning of the word צו here. Rashi tells us that, not only here but in other places as well, the word צו carries its own, independent, message. It means: "I urge you to do these commandments immediately and for generations." This *drash* is understandable, since "to command" implies a more demanding request than do the words "to say to." Certainly "commanding" is appropriate when the person commanded might dally because he doesn't see the urgency of the command or because implementing it will entail a monetary loss.

"Said Rabbi Shimon"

Rabbi Shimon says the word צו is particularly apt when a loss of money is involved. Does Rabbi Shimon disagree with the first opinion or is he just making an additional comment?

YOUR ANSWER:

An Answer: There is a rule of thumb which teaches us whether two opinions of the Sages are antagonistic or complementary. When the second opinion is introduced, as in our case, with "Said Rabbi Shimon" that is, when the verb ("said") comes before the name ("Rabbi Shimon"), it means only that the Sage, Rabbi Shimon, offers another, alternative interpretation but not that he necessarily disagrees with the first opinion. But, if it were to say "Rabbi Shimon said" when the name comes before the verb ("said"), then we assume that he disagrees with the previous opinion.

"A Monetary Loss"

This phrase has caused much discussion among the commentaries. What monetary loss does the priest have here? Can you think of an answer?

YOUR ANSWER:

Understanding Rashi

Many have attempted to understand the meaning of Rabbi Shimon's statement.

1) Some say this refers to the burnt offering which is discussed in this section. The burnt offering is totally consumed on the alter. The priest receives nothing from it (as he does in other offerings) except the skin, which was not considered of much value.

   So he has to do all the work of sacrificing it with little in return. The Ramban does not agree with this. He apparently considers the skin to be worthwhile payment.

2) The Ramban suggests that this refers to the High Priest's own offering mentioned later (6:13ff) This meal offering is paid for by the priest but is totally consumed by the alter and he has no personal gratification from it.

3) Another interpretation given is that the priests offer the sacrifices for their brother Israelites, and if the priests have a wrong intention while preparing the offering, the sacrifice is invalidated. The need for the priest to replace the invalidated offering, could be the loss that Rabbi Shimon is referring to.

   Can you suggest your own answer?

   Hint: Read carefully the first four verses in this section.

YOUR ANSWER:

My Answer: If we read these verses carefully we see that the main instruction
given to the priest here is that he should take out the ashes. When
he performs this mitzvah he must be wearing his priestly garments.
By carrying the ashes outside the camp, he may sully his beautiful
white linen garments. Because of that he must have a second pair
ready to change into. (See the next Rashi analysis.) I would suggest that this is the monetary loss Rabbi Shimon refers to.

(See *Ramban, Sefer Zikaron*)

*What are reasonable inferences from the Torah's words? Rashi and
Ramban differ.*

Leviticus 6:4

וּפָשַׁט אֶת־בְּגָדָיו וְלָבַשׁ בְּגָדִים אֲחֵרִים וְהוֹצִיא אֶת־הַדֶּשֶׁן אֶל מִחוּץ
לַמַּחֲנֶה אֶל מָקוֹם טָהוֹר.

וּפָשַׁט אֶת בְּגָדָיו. אֵין זוֹ חוֹבָה אֶלָּא דֶּרֶךְ אֶרֶץ. שֶׁלֹּא יְלַכְלֵךְ
בְּהוֹצָאַת הַדֶּשֶׁן בְּגָדִים שֶׁהוּא מְשַׁמֵּשׁ בָּהֶם תָּמִיד. בְּגָדִים שֶׁבִּשֵּׁל
בָּהֶם קְדֵרָה לְרַבּוֹ אַל יִמְזוֹג בָּהֶן כּוֹס לְרַבּוֹ, לְכָךְ **וְלָבַשׁ בְּגָדִים
אֲחֵרִים**, פְּחוּתִים מֵהֶם.

And he shall remove his garments: *Rashi*: This is not
obligatory, it is rather a matter of proper conduct so that
he should not, through removing the ashes, soil the garments in which he constantly serves [at the altar]. 'The
clothes [he wore] when he boiled the pot for his master
he should not pour [while still dressed] in them a cup of
wine for his master.' On this account it states **'and he
shall put on other garments'** — inferior to those [in
which he constantly serves at the altar].

WHAT IS RASHI SAYING ?

The Torah tells us that the priest must change his clothes when he removes the ashes from the altar to outside the camp, but does not tell us

the reason for this changing of clothes. Note: There are two acts here. One is called *terumas hadeshen* which is described in verse 6:3. There the priest takes a small amount of ashes daily from the altar and places them at the side of the altar. For this he dons the priest's special linen clothes. This act alone will not sully him or his clothing, thus he need not change his garments. But the next step is to remove the large pile of ashes from the altar to outside the camp. This is like collecting garbage and will almost certainly dirty the priest's clothes. He is therefore explicitly instructed to change into other clothes.

Note that while the Torah tells the priest to change his clothes, no reason is given for this. Rashi supplies the rationale for changing clothes, i.e., that he should not sully his good garments.

The Torah only says he must change into other garments; Rashi tells us that the change of clothing is to *inferior* clothing.

What does he mean by this? Does he mean inferior quality priestly garments or does he mean ordinary, non-priestly garments, which are, by definition, inferior?

Hint: If you read carefully this verse you should see the answer.

YOUR ANSWER:

"INFERIOR GARMENTS"

An Answer: The Torah says "He shall remove his garments and don other garments."

Of course, if he removes his clothes he must put on other clothes. He wouldn't walk around the Temple naked! So, the second part of the verse can't mean to wear non-priestly garments, that would be too obvious to need mentioning. On the basis of this inference, Rashi concludes that if these words were used, they must teach us something. The priest must put on other *garments* (similar to the *garments* he took off, i.e. priestly *garments*). But if so why would he switch from priestly garments to other priestly garments? What benefit is there in that? Thus Rashi concludes, these must be priestly garments but of inferior (used) quality.

A CLOSER LOOK

But if Rashi's whole point is that he don other clothing, then his *dibbur hamaschil* — "and he shall remove his garments" — chooses the wrong words. A more appropriate *dibbur hamaschil* would have been the next words, "and he shall don other garments." How do you understand this?

Hint: Look carefully at Rashi's full comment.

YOUR ANSWER:

A Closer Understanding

An Answer: Rashi has done clever editorial work here. He has inserted another *dibbur hamaschil* toward the end of this comment when he says: "On this account it states 'and he shall put on other garments' — inferior to those [in which he regularly serves at the altar]."

Here he quotes those words of the Torah which are relevant for his comment. We can now understand that the main point of Rashi's comment is to tell us the reason for the priest's need to change clothes (something the Torah does not tell us). Rashi gives us the meaning for changing clothes under the *dibbur hamaschil* "And he shall remove his garments." Then he gives the analogy, and only then, under the inserted *dibbur hamaschil*, "and he shall don other garments" does he comment on the meaning of these apparently superfluous words. They are not superfluous, for they teach us that the "other" garments, are priestly garments, though they should be of inferior quality.

Ramban's Dispute With Rashi

The Ramban takes issue with Rashi on his statement that "this (changing clothes) is not obligatory, just a matter of דרך ארץ — good conduct." The Ramban says:

> "....But I don't know whence the Rav (Rashi) says that this is not obligatory. Because it seems that it is a mitzvah (obligation) for the priest, that the garments he wears should be clean when he offers the sacrifices, as well as when he takes the *teruma* of the ashes. He should not use them when he takes the ashes [outside the camp]. The mitzvah is by way of discipline of the servant towards his master. Therefore the priests should have appealing garments for the actual service and inferior garments for taking out the ashes..."

It is clear that the Ramban disagrees with Rashi. It seems that he believes this is a mitzvah because the Torah says explicitly "he should remove his garments and don other garments."

How would you defend Rashi's position, that this is not a mitzvah, just an act of good conduct?

Hint: Look at the verse here and understand clearly what it says.

YOUR ANSWER:

DEFENDING RASHI

An Answer: All the Torah says is that the priest should remove his clothes and don other clothes before he takes out the ashes. The Torah says nothing regarding which clothes the priest should wear *after* he takes out the ashes (and possibly has dirtied them). If there were an obligatory act involved here, it should be regarding the clothes he wears afterwards. It doesn't make too much sense to say that the whole mitzvah is to wear inferior clothes when he take out the ashes. The point is that the next time he serves *Hashem* at the altar, he should be wearing clean clothes — and that is not mentioned in the verse at all. So Rashi seems to have a point that what the verse says here about the clothes the priest wears when he takes the ashes out, is not a mitzvah. It is rather of the order of proper conduct, that he should be concerned that when he serves his master the next time his clothes should be unsullied.

I can think of another answer to defend Rashi's opinion that the changing of clothes is not obligatory.

Can you?

YOUR ANSWER:

An Answer: We have many objects of mitzvah in the Torah — tefillin, tzitzis, succah, shofar, even esrog. In none of them is there an *obligation* that they must be beautiful beyond the basic requirements of the mitzvah, and if they are not, they are invalid. Why then should the priest's garments be any different? Of course they should be beautiful and clean, but they are not invalidated, as the Ramban seems to say, if they are neither beautiful nor clean.

But we are not yet finished analyzing this comment.

Rashi's Parable

Look at the parable of the servant and his master. Is it parallel to our situation here?

What would you ask?

Your Question:

Questioning Rashi

A Question: Rashi's parable of the servant who first boils a pot for his master and later serves him wine, seems backwards. Boiling the pot is analogous to removing the ashes (both are tasks which dirty one's clothing); serving the wine is analogous to offering a sacrifice at the altar (both are acts of offering something directly to the master). But in our verse the priest has already offered the sacrifice — the ashes are the remnants of that sacrifice! So the 'dirty work' comes *after* the more dignified work of serving the master. The analogy seems to be backwards.

Why did Rashi use it?

Your Answer:

Understanding Rashi

An Answer: Of course, looked at in that way the parable is backwards. But the analogy simply means that once the priest has dirtied his clothes by taking out the ashes, he cannot use them *again in the future* to offer other sacrifices, since he has already sullied them. In the words of the analogy, he can *no longer* serve wine to the master since he has already boiled a pot while wearing these clothes and in so doing he has dirtied them.

Rashi was aware of this question; he avoided the problem by adding one word. Which word did he add which deftly makes the parable appropriate?

Your Answer:

A CLOSER LOOK

An Answer: Rashi says "garments in which he **constantly** serves..." "בגדים שישמש בהם **תמיד**" By adding the word תמיד Rashi makes it clear that he is thinking of the priest's work on a regular basis, and not just what he did earlier before he took out the ashes, but also what he will do tomorrow after he has taken out the ashes.

(See *Sefer Zicharon, Ramban* and *Lubavitcher.*)

❖❖❖

A puzzling comment that is a brainteaser. This is really a complex Rashi-comment. But I like it because it shows how sensitive Rashi is to the subtleties of the Torah's language.

Leviticus 6:15

וְהַכֹּהֵן הַמָּשִׁיחַ תַּחְתָּיו מִבָּנָיו יַעֲשֶׂה אֹתָהּ חָק־עוֹלָם לַה' כָּלִיל תָּקְטָר.

המשיח תחתיו מבניו. המשיח מבניו תחתיו.
Who is anointed [המשיח] in his stead, from his sons.
Rashi: Who is anointed [המשיח] of his sons, in his stead.

WHAT HAS RASHI DONE?

This is a very strange comment, its strangeness is more obvious in the original Hebrew.

The Torah says "המשיח תחתיו מבניו". Rashi adds nothing to the Torah's words; he only re-arranges them and says: "המשיח מבניו תחתיו". In English the two versions look like this:

The Torah's version: "And the כהן המשיח *in his stead, of his sons,* shall perform it" etc.

Rashi's version: "And the כהן המשיח *of his sons, in his stead,* shall perform it" etc.

Why has he done this?

In order to analyze and understand this very subtle Rashi-comment, we must first provide some background.

What Is the Verse Speaking About?

Our verse is a continuation of the laws which began in verse 13. There it tells us that on the first day of a newly installed High Priest he is to bring a special meal-offering.

Our verse tells us that the same offering is brought by each succeeding High Priest (who is chosen from among the sons of the previous High Priest) on the day of his installation.

Questioning Rashi

The obvious question is: Why does Rashi make the switch in word order?

Can you make sense out of this puzzling comment?

Your Answer:

Understanding Rashi

Some additional information is necessary to make sense of Rashi. The words in Hebrew "הכהן המשיח" can have two slightly different meanings. The word "המשיח" can mean either:

1) The one who is anointed. In that case it is a passive verb,

or :

2) The Anointed-One (as we use the word *Mashiach*). In that case it is a noun, a title.

Rashi takes the word as a noun, like a title, i.e., the Priest, the Anointed-One or in Hebrew it is one-name-phrase: "The כהן-המשיח."

Now let us read the verse according to Rashi:

"And הכהן המשיח, from his sons, in his stead" etc.

This makes better sense than the order in the Torah:

"And הכהן המשיח in his stead, from his sons..." In order to have these words make sense, we would have to add the words (in italics): " And כהן המשיח *who is appointed* in his stead, from his sons."

So Rashi indirectly tells us to translate the word המשיח as a noun, (the *Mashiach*) and thus he must change the order of the words of the Torah to have them make the best sense.

But then you should have a serious question to ask of Rashi.

YOUR QUESTION:

A Serious Question _____

If Rashi's order is the best, then why doesn't the Torah use that order, instead of the order it has? Why does the Torah say "The *cohen-mashiach* in his stead, of his sons"? This is awkward.

This is a difficult question. Some help can be derived from another Rashi-comment. On the verse in Exodus 29:30, we have a similar Rashi-comment. Look it up. Maybe it can shed some light on this question.

YOUR ANSWER:

A Deeper Understanding _____

There Rashi says the true, basic meaning of the word כהן means "to work" or "to serve." It is a verb which also can be used as a noun. We are most familiar with the word כהן as a noun, meaning a person of the priestly family. A word having two meanings, one as a noun the other as a verb, is similar to a word like "שומר", which means "watchman." But it is also a verb, "הוא שומר" means "he watches."

Perhaps, in a way similar to כהן and שומר, Rashi uses the word משיח as a noun, because he realizes that this is the way it is commonly understood. So he makes his comment on the basis of how we, the student of the *chumash*, would understand it. However, the real, original, meaning of the word is "the one who is anointed." (As Rashi had said about the word "יכהן" "one who serves.") Therefore, the Torah, itself, uses the word משיח in its basic sense, which means "the one who is anointed." Thus the appropriate phrase is "The *cohen* who is anointed (המשיח) in his stead, from his sons."

Reconciling Rashi's Word Order with the Torah's Words _____

Thus, the Torah's order is correct, because it uses the word in its original, basic sense, as a verb ("the one who is anointed"); and Rashi's order is correct because he uses it as a noun, since that is its familiar meaning ("the anointed-one"), in order that the student can more easily understand the verse.

(See *Havanas Hamikra*)

A complex comment which must be analyzed particle by particle. It shows Rashi's precise choice of words and how he reworks a midrash.

Leviticus 7:12

אִם עַל־תּוֹדָה יַקְרִיבֶנּוּ וְהִקְרִיב עַל־זֶבַח הַתּוֹדָה חַלּוֹת מַצּוֹת בְּלוּלֹת
בַּשֶּׁמֶן וּרְקִיקֵי מַצּוֹת מְשֻׁחִים בַּשָּׁמֶן וְסֹלֶת מֻרְבֶּכֶת חַלֹּת בְּלוּלֹת
בַּשָּׁמֶן.

אם על תודה יקריבנו. אִם עַל דְּבַר הוֹדָאָה, עַל נֵס שֶׁנַּעֲשָׂה לוֹ —
כְּגוֹן יוֹרְדֵי הַיָּם וְהוֹלְכֵי מִדְבָּרוֹת וַחֲבוּשֵׁי בֵית הָאֲסוּרִים וְחוֹלֶה
שֶׁנִּתְרַפֵּא — שֶׁהֵם צְרִיכִין לְהוֹדוֹת, שֶׁכָּתוּב בָּהֶן "יוֹדוּ לַה׳ חַסְדּוֹ
וְנִפְלְאוֹתָיו לִבְנֵי אָדָם וְיִזְבְּחוּ זִבְחֵי תוֹדָה" (תהילים קז:כא) —
אִם עַל אַחַת מֵאֵלֶּה נָדַר שְׁלָמִים הַלָּלוּ, שַׁלְמֵי תוֹדָה הֵן, וּטְעוּנוֹת
לֶחֶם הָאָמוּר בָּעִנְיָן וְאֵין נֶאֱכָלִין אֶלָּא לְיוֹם וָלַיְלָה כְּמוֹ שֶׁמְּפוֹרָשׁ
כָּאן.

If he offers it as a thanksgiving. *Rashi:* If [he brings it] on account of a matter of thanksgiving — on a miracle that happened to him, for example, those who go down to the sea, those who travel in the desert, those who are imprisoned or he who was sick and recovered, they are required to thank [G-d] as it says of them "Let them give thanks to *Hashem* for His kindness and His wonders to the children of men. And let them slaughter thanksgiving offerings..." — if on account of one of these things he vowed these peace offerings, they are "peace offerings for thanksgiving" and require the [addition of] breads that are mentioned in the section and may not be eaten beyond a period of one day and one night, as is explained here.

WHAT IS RASHI SAYING ? _____

What Rashi says, essentially, is that this is a special "peace offering" for those occasions when a person survived a dangerous situation and is required to thank *Hashem* for His help. But this is a relatively long comment. To best understand it let us see Rashi's emphasis and thrust in his explanation. He tells us several different things:

1) He tells us that *if* a man makes an offering due to his thankfulness,

2) It is called a "Peace offering of Thanksgiving."

3) This offering has special laws, i.e., the additional breads and the time limitation in eating them.

4) And almost in passing, he mentions four examples of survival situations which require this offering.

Why all this? Is it all necessary to understanding the verse?

YOUR ANSWER:

WHAT IS RASHI CLARIFYING?

An Answer: Rashi is making order out of the verses in this section (7:11-21) which tell of the laws of the *Shelamim* — "peace offering." (See verse 7:11.) There are two different types of *Shelamim* mentioned here. The first (the Thanksgiving offering) is described in our verses 7:12-15. The second (the Vow) is described later in verses 7:16-18. Now notice that the first clause in our verse 7:12 is conditional, beginning with the word "If." The question is: What is conditional on what?

YOUR ANSWER:

BEGINNING TO UNDERSTAND RASHI

An Answer: There is a likely misunderstanding here. I might have understood the words על תודה to mean "for a Thanksgiving offering." But this cannot be correct. If it were correct then it would read: "If he offers a Thanksgiving offering, then he shall offer it..." This is obviously redundant. Therefore Rashi tells us point #1 above; the words על תודה mean "for a [feeling of] thanksgiving" and not "for an offering of thanksgiving." We can now understand the conditional clause: If a person has a feeling of thanksgiving towards G-d, *then* he should give the special offering called זבח התודה "the offering of thanksgiving."

If we scrutinize Rashi's words, we see that he parallels and clarifies the Torah's words.

The Torah's words	Rashi's words
אם **עַל** תודה	אם על דבר הודאה
If with a thanksgiving offering	If regarding a matter of thanksgiving
והקריב **עַל** זבח התודה	שלמי תודה הן
And he shall bring together with the thanksgiving offering	they are peace offerings of thanksgiving
חלות מצות בלולת וגו'	וטעונות לחם האמור בענין
matzoh loaves mixed etc.	and they require bread as is said here

Note that the first על means "regarding." The second על means "with."

A Close Look at Rashi and the *Midrash*

Now we come to a most fascinating part of this comment. When we look at it closely, we see how Rashi used his genius to craft his exemplary commentary. Rashi inserted the additional note, that there are four survivors who need to bring this sacrifice. Rashi's source is the Talmud *Berachos* 54b. Let us compare Rashi's source in the Talmud with his own words.

The source:

> "Rav Yehuda said in the name of Rav: Four need to thank [G-d]. Those who go down to [sail] the sea; those who travel in the desert; he who is sick and recovers; and he who was imprisoned and was freed..."

As evidence that is so, extensive quotation from Psalms 107 is cited. These four cases are mentioned and after each case it repeats the phrase: "Let them give thanks to *Hashem* for His kindness and His wonders for the children of man."

Following are excerpts from psalm 107:

4. They wandered in the wilderness in the desolation of the path; they found no inhabited city.	ד. תעו במדבר בישימון דרך עיר מושב לא מצאו.
6. Then they cried out to *Hashem* in their distress He would rescue them from their straits.	ו. ויצעקו אל ה' בצר להם ממצוקותיהם יצילם.
8. Let them give thanks to *Hashem* for His kindness and His wonders to the children of man.	ח. יודו לה' חסדו ונפלאותיו לבני אדם.
10. Those who sat in darkness and the shadow of death, shackled in affliction and iron.	י. ישבי חושך וצלמות אסירי עני וברזל.

יג. ויזעקו אל ה' בצר להם 13. Then they cried out to *Hashem* in their distress,
ממצקותיהם יושיעם. He would save them from their straits.
טו. יודו לה' חסדו 15. Let them give thanks to *Hashem* for His kindness
ונפלאותיו לבני אדם. and His wonders to the children of man.

יח. כל אכל תתעב נפשם 18. Their soul abhorred all food
ויגיעו עד שערי מות. and they reached unto the portals of death.
יט. ויזעקו אל ה' בצר להם 19. Then they cried out to *Hashem* in their distress,
ממצקותיהם יושיעם. He would save them from their straits.
כא. יודו לה' חסדו 21. Let them give thanks to *Hashem* for His kindness
ונפלאותיו לבני אדם. and His wonders to the children of man.
כב. ויזבחו זבחי תודה 22. And let them slaughter thanksgiving offerings,
ויספרו מעשיו ברנה. and relate His works with joyful song.

כג. יורדי הים באניות 23. Those who go down to the sea in ships,
עשי מלאכה במים רבים. who do their work in great waters
כח. ויצעקו אל ה' בצר להם 28. Then they cried out to *Hashem* in their distress,
וממצוקתיהם יוציאם. He would save them from their straits.
לא. יודו לה' חסדו 31. Let them give thanks to *Hashem* for His kindness
ונפלאותיו לבני אדם. and His wonders to the children of man.

From these verses we can see clearly the source in Psalms for the halachic interpretation of what Rav Yehuda said in the name of Rav.

Now compare Rashi's words about these four cases with the four cases of Rav. Look closely. Do you see any differences between them?

What differences?

Enumerate them.

Your Answer:

The Differences _____

I. The order is not the same.

Rav	**Rashi**
1) seafarers	1) seafarers
2) desert travelers	2) desert travelers
3) one recovered from illness	3) released prisoners
4) released prisoner	4) one recovered from illness

See that Rashi reverses Rav's #3 and #4.

II.   Another difference: Rav has both #3 and #4 in the singular, while Rashi has all three cases in plural except for the one who recovers from an illness, that he phrases in the singular.

III.   Yet another difference: Rashi introduces the four survivors with the words "if a miracle happens to them..." Rav doesn't mention the term miracle.

Can you make sense out of these differences?

YOUR ANSWER:

UNDERSTANDING RASHI'S RESHAPING THE *MIDRASH*

I.   Rashi's point in his comment on the Torah's words is to explain that the four survivors must bring the זבח תודה. Psalm 107, which is the source of Rav's *drash* repeats the words "Let them give thanks to *Hashem* for His kindness ..." four times. But — and this is the crucial point — only once does it add the words "Let them give thanks to *Hashem*...and let them slaughter thanksgiving offerings זבחי תודה." This one and only time comes after the recovery of the ill man is mentioned! Thus Rashi cites the ill man last to connect this with the relevant and crucial words from Psalms — זבחי תודה ויזבחו. We see that Rashi ties in his last case with this idea of the offering: וחולה שנתרפא – שהם צריכין להודות.

Since Rashi's whole point is to explain this verse in the Torah which teaches us when individuals have to bring a thanksgiving offering, he had to link up the idea of thanksgiving to the idea of bringing an offering. He did this by changing the Talmudic order and placing the sick who was healed next to his comment "these must give thanksgiving," since only with the recovered person is the phrase of bringing an offering mentioned in Psalms. We really see here Rashi's brilliant originality in his commentary. His nearly imperceptible switch allows him to make the Sage's *midrashic* interpretation reasonable, understandable, and relevant to the Torah's words.

II.   Why does Rashi phrase only the case of the recovered ill in the singular? Rav has both the prisoner and the recovered ill in the singular.

An Answer: Of the four dangers that are mentioned, three of them usually happen to more than one person at a time (sailing in a boat, traveling in the desert, being thrown into jail). But being sick is a singularly individual experience. If the boat is saved, all may be rescued, but someone else's recovery from an illness in no way affects my recovery. It is my own very personal danger. Thus Rashi uses the singular only in the case of the ill person.

III.   Rashi refers to these redemptions from danger as "miracles." Rashi's use of the term "miracle" (which is not taken from the *midrash*) when speaking of salvation based on normal, natural, events shows us his appreciation for what is called a "hidden miracle." These are discussed by the Ramban in Exodus 13:16 where he explains that behind all events there is a divine guiding hand. Some salvations are striking in that they go against the laws of nature, while others work within the laws of nature. This difference is one of "quantity" and not one of "quality," not one of more or less divine intervention. All events are the result of divine "intervention."

A classic Type II comment, shows how Rashi diffuses a possible misunderstanding.

Leviticus 7:16

וְאִם־נֶדֶר אוֹ נְדָבָה זֶבַח קָרְבָּנוֹ בְּיוֹם הַקְרִיבוֹ אֶת־זִבְחוֹ יֵאָכֵל וּמִמָּחֳרָת וְהַנּוֹתָר מִמֶּנּוּ יֵאָכֵל.

וממחרת והנותר ממנו. בראשון יֵאכל. ויו זו יתירה היא, ויש כמוה הרבה במקרא כגון ואלה בני צבעון ואיה וענה (בראשית לו:כד) תת וקדש וצבא מרמס (דניאל ח:יג).

And on the morrow and the remainder of it: *Rashi*: On the first day, **may be eaten**. This letter **ו** is redundant. There are many similar examples in Scripture, for example "and these are the sons of Zibeon, (and) Ayah and Anah" (Genesis 36:24) "allows that which is (and) holy, and the host to be trampled." (Daniel 8:13)

This is a prime example of a Type II Rashi-comment. See how he inserts one word — "on the first day" — and then continues with the word from the verse itself "may be eaten." This means that Rashi is guarding us from misinterpreting the verse.

What possible misinterpretation is he guarding us from?

YOUR ANSWER:

What Possible Misinterpretation?

An Answer: If we read the verse as it is written, we would likely have understood it in the following way:

"...it shall be eaten 1) on the day of his offering and 2) on the next day,
and 3) the remnant of it may be eaten." Which is to say that one may eat
the sacrifice on the day it is offered, on the next day and then (on the
third day) that which remains may also be eaten. When may it also be
eaten? On the day after the day after the offering, i.e., on the third day.
So this offering maybe eaten, if necessary, for three days.

But Rashi rejects this interpretation. Why?

Hint: Read the verses in this section.

Your Answer:

Understanding Rashi

An Answer: Rashi must interpret the verse as he does because of the following
verse. There it says: "Whatever meat of the offering is left over —
והנותר — shall be burnt in fire on the third day." So, the Torah
clearly states that the remnant cannot be eaten on the third day; for
it must be burnt.

Therefore, Rashi interprets the verse to mean that the remnant can
be eaten on the morrow "of the first day" (not "the remnant of the
morrow" of the second day).

But there is a problem with this interpretation. If we translate the verse
exactly as it is written, it does not seem to coincide with Rashi's interpretation. Rashi had to make a change to have his interpretation accord
with the Torah's words.

What change did he make and why?

Your Answer:

A Closer Look

An Answer: In the second part of this comment, Rashi tells us that the letter ו in
the word ו הנותר ("**and** the remnant") is superfluous. The meaning
is not "it shall be eaten and on the morrow, **and** the remnant of it

shall be eaten." This would imply three days of eating. The correct translation Rashi tells us, is, (without the second "and") thus: "it should be eaten, and on the morrow the remnant of it shall be eaten." Only with this change can we understand that the "remnant" referred to here is food that remained from the first day and not from the second day.

(See Mizrachi, Sefer Zikaron)

Sensitivity to subtleties in the Torah-text teaches us something about the Priestly blessing.

Leviticus 9:22

וַיִּשָּׂא אַהֲרֹן אֶת־יָדוֹ אֶל־הָעָם וַיְבָרְכֵם וַיֵּרֶד מֵעֲשֹׂת הַחַטָּאת וְהָעֹלָה וְהַשְּׁלָמִים.

וִיבָרְכֵם. ברכת כהנים, יברכך, יאר, ישא.
And he blessed them: *Rashi:* The Priestly blessing. 'May [*Hashem*] bless you', 'may [*Hashem*] shine', 'may [*Hashem*] raise up'.

Some fundamental questions can be asked here.

Your Questions:

Questioning Rashi

A Question: How does Rashi know that this blessing is the Priestly blessing?

The Priestly blessing is commanded in Numbers 6:23ff. There it says:

> "Speak unto Aaron and his sons, saying: So shall you shall bless the Children of Israel, saying to them:
> 'May *Hashem* bless you and guard you.
> May *Hashem* shine His countenance to you and grace you.
> May *Hashem* raise up His countenance to you and give you peace.' "

With this blessing in mind, can you see how Rashi concluded that Aaron's blessing here was the same Priestly blessing?

This is not easy.

Your Answer:

How Does Rashi Know?

An Answer: The Priestly blessing has a unique feature which is rarely noticed: The people are blessed directly in the second person, as the priest faces them and speaks to them face to face. He says " May *Hashem* bless **you**" "and grace **you**," and "and give **you** peace." This accords with our verse which says: "And Aaron raised his hands *toward the people*." This indicates clearly that he faced the people and blessed them directly, indicating the unique characteristic of the Priestly blessing.

In order to see the uniqueness of such a frontal blessing, let us compare it with Solomon's blessing to the people when the first Temple was dedicated. Our verse also refers to a holy dedication, i.e. the special ceremonies on the day when the Tabernacle was dedicated.

"He (Solomon) stood and blessed the entire congregation of Israel in a loud voice saying: 'Blessed is *Hashem* Who has granted rest to His people Israel." (I Kings 8:55).

Notice that this is not a blessing to the people, it is a blessing (thanksgiving) to *Hashem* and only indirectly a blessing for the people. Aaron's Priestly blessing, on the other hand, is one directed to the people themselves.

Another Question

Why does Rashi give us the first words of the blessing? We certainly know what the Priestly blessing is.

Your Answer:

Understanding Rashi

An Answer: These words, particularly the first — יברכך — is a clue to the fact that the blessing is a direct one, since in each of the three phrases the people are addressed directly in the second person.

A Deeper Look

Some commentaries on Rashi have suggested that Rashi knew this was the Priestly blessing because it says here "And Aaron *raised his hands*." And raising the hands is indicative of the Priestly blessing. But this answer is problematic. Can you see why?

Hint: Look again at the Priestly blessing above.

YOUR ANSWER:

An Answer: The section regarding the Priestly blessing says nothing about the raising of the hands. The law of the priest raising his hands in blessing is derived from our verse! Because Aaron raised his hands here and blessed the people, we know that the priest must raise his hands when he blesses the people.

AND YET ANOTHER QUESTION

A Question: The Priestly blessing was commanded to Aaron later on in the book of Numbers. How could Aaron have used it now, before he was commanded concerning it?

    Hint: Look closely at that section in Numbers and the context in which it occurs.

YOUR ANSWER:

An Answer: The verse immediately following the Priestly blessing (Numbers 7:1) says "And it was on the day that Moses finished setting up the Tabernacle" etc. Rashi on that verse tells us that this took place on *Rosh Chodesh* Nisan. We know that the events in our *parasha* also took place on that same *Rosh Chodesh* Nisan, as Rashi tells us on the first verse in this sedra (Leviticus 9:1). So both events took place at the same time. It would thus seem that, in fact, Aaron was given the instructions about the Priestly blessings at the time of the dedication of the Tabernacle. So he already knew these blessings by the time he blessed the people in our verse.

                                      (See *Be'er Basadeh; Biurim L'pirush Rashi*)

Rashi chooses the midrash to fit the verse.

Leviticus 10:1,2

וַיִּקְחוּ בְנֵי־אַהֲרֹן נָדָב וַאֲבִיהוּא אִישׁ מַחְתָּתוֹ וַיִּתְּנוּ בָהֵן אֵשׁ וַיָּשִׂימוּ
עָלֶיהָ קְטֹרֶת וַיַּקְרִיבוּ לִפְנֵי ה' אֵשׁ זָרָה אֲשֶׁר לֹא צִוָּה אֹתָם. וַתֵּצֵא
אֵשׁ מִלִּפְנֵי ה' וַתֹּאכַל אוֹתָם וַיָּמֻתוּ לִפְנֵי ה'.

וַתֵּצֵא אֵשׁ. ר' אליעזר אומר לא מתו בני אהרן אלא על ידי
שהורו הלכה בפני משה רבן. רבי ישמעאל אומר שתויי יין
נכנסו למקדש. תדע שאחר מיתתן הזהיר הנותרים שלא יכנסו
שתויי יין למקדש. משל למלך שהיה לו בן בית וכו' כדאיתא
בויקרא רבה.

And fire came forth: *Rashi:* Rabbi Eliezer says: The sons
of Aaron died only because they rendered halachic deci-
sions in the presence of their teacher Moses. Rabbi
Yishmael says: [They died because] they entered the Sanctuary while intoxicated with wine. You can know that this
is so, because after their death [G-d] warned the survivors not to enter the Sanctuary while intoxicated by wine
(See this chapter, verses 8-11). This may be compared to
a king who had a faithful member of his household etc.
as it is found in *Vayikra Rabbah*.

Rashi gives us two possible reasons for the sudden deaths of Nadav and
Avihu.

What questions would you ask on this comment?

YOUR QUESTIONS:

QUESTIONING RASHI

A Question: Rashi supplies us with reasons for the death of Aaron's sons, but
the Torah itself says "and they brought before *Hashem* a strange
fire which He commanded them not." This would seem to be the
reason for their deaths. Why does Rashi need to suggest other reasons?

You may remember other instances in the Torah where Rashi offers reasons for events when the Torah itself had already stated a reason. See,
for example, Rashi's comments on the case of Yisro's coming to meet
Moses (Exodus 18:1) and on the naming of Reuben (Genesis 29:32). In
each case, Rashi offers reasons other than those which the Torah itself

gives. His comment alerts us to closely search the words of the Torah to discover subtleties which prompted Rashi's comment.

Can you find the reason for Rashi's comment here?

What's bothering Rashi?

YOUR ANSWER:

WHAT IS BOTHERING RASHI ?

An Answer: An explanation for the need for additional reasons for the deaths of Nadav and Avihu may be that they had done something apparently quite positive. They brought a voluntary offering to G-d. Why should they be punished — and with such a sever punishment — for a well-intentioned act?

With this in mind, how does Rashi's comment deal with this difficulty in the verse?

YOUR ANSWER:

UNDERSTANDING RASHI

An Answer: Rashi's comment is meant to explain how the sin of these men was deserving of the death penalty. Bringing the strange fire was an unintentional transgression; but deciding the law in Moses' presence was an intentional act which flaunted the chain of authority in halachic matters. Also entering the Tabernacle in an intoxicated state is a flagrant violation of the decorum of such a holy place The death penalty, harsh as it was, can more easily be appreciated with the additional reasons that Rashi offers us.

QUESTIONING RABBI ELIEZER'S EXPLANATION

On what basis do you think that Rabbi Eliezer concluded that their sin was deciding the halacha without consulting Moses?

Hint: Look carefully at the verse.

YOUR ANSWER:

UNDERSTANDING THE *MIDRASH*

An Answer: The Torah says "*Hashem* had not commanded *them* to bring." The extra word "them" implies that *Hashem* had commanded to bring this fire, but had not commanded *them* to do so. If so, Moses, the Lawgiver, would have to decide who should be the one to bring this fire. But they brought it without being commanded. The fact that they did bring the fire shows that they decided to do so without consulting the leading authority of the generation (of all generations, for that matter !), Moses, their teacher.

See above 1:7 (*parashas* Vayikra) where it says that the sons of Aaron are to put fire on the altar. There Rashi notes "Even though fire would come down from heaven it was nevertheless a *mitzvah* for 'profane' fire to be brought [by the priests]." So it seems that Nadav and Avihu weren't doing anything wrong. However, since Moses had not ordered them to be the ones to bring this fire, they had acted out of turn.

RABBI YISHMAEL'S EXPLANATION

The reason for Rabbi Yishmael's interpretation is clear. Rashi himself says that the fact that immediately after this tragedy, G-d commanded Aaron not to enter the Sanctuary intoxicated by wine, would indicate that intoxication was the reason for Nadav and Avihu's death, as the parable points out.

But you should have a question on this interpretation of Rabbi Yishmael.

YOUR QUESTION:

QUESTIONING RABBI YISHMAEL

A Question: If G-d only forbade entering the Sanctuary in a state of intoxication *after* the deaths of Nadav and Avihu, why were *they* punished. At the time they entered the Sanctuary intoxicated, there was as yet no prohibition.

YOUR ANSWER:

UNDERSTANDING RABBI YISHMAEL

An Answer: Common sense and common decency would dictate — even without a divine edict — that one should not enter such a holy place while under the influence of wine. They should have understood this themselves. They are no less responsible for their irresponsible behavior just because they were not told explicitly of this prohibition. However, once G-d saw that they could ignore this elementary act of decency, He found it necessary to make the law explicit and abundantly clear. So afterwards He made a formal declaration to Aaron of the laws of decorum when serving in the Sanctuary.

RASHI AND *MIDRASH*

Rashi here cites two *midrashic* interpretations for the deaths of Nadav and Avihu. But those familiar with Rashi throughout the Torah may recall that in other places he has given other reasons for their deaths.

See Exodus 24:9. On the words "They saw the G-d of Israel," Rashi says:

> "They looked and peeked and were guilty of death. But [G-d] did not want to dilute the joy of Receiving the Torah so He waited [to punish Nadav and Avihu] until the day of the dedication of the Tabernacle.

See also Leviticus 10:12. On the words "Elazar and Itamar, his remaining sons," Rashi says:

> "[Those that survived] death. This teaches us that they too were to have been punished by death for the sin of the Golden Calf."

And see Leviticus 16:1. On the words "And *Hashem* spoke to Moses after the death of the two sons of Aaron," Rashi says:

> "Rabbi Eliezer son of Azariah suggested a parable: of a sick man whom the doctor visited etc. ...Therefore it says 'after the deaths of the two sons of Aaron.' "

The reference is to the Torah's words "after the death of the two sons of Aaron *when they came near to Hashem* and they died." Rabbi Eliezer, son of Azariah, thus concludes that they died because they "came near to *Hashem*."

We see that in different places in his Torah commentary, Rashi has offered five different reasons for the deaths of Nadav and Avihu. Why does he cite so many different and contradictory reasons? And if he does find the need to cite them, why does he cite one reason in one place and in another place he cites another reason? How are we to understand this?

Can you explain it?

YOUR ANSWER:

RASHI'S METHOD WITH *MIDRASH*

This example teaches us an important lesson about Rashi's use of *midrashim*. Many *midrashim* exist; many, many more than Rashi cites, as he himself tells us in his famous programmatic statement in Genesis 3:8. But Rashi cites only those *midrashim* that have relevance to the particular verse he is commenting on. Rashi selects the *midrashic* explanation that best fits in with the particular context within which their deaths are mentioned. In our case, he cites two opinions for the deaths of Nadav and Avihu.

It is important to point out that Rashi drew the first opinion, that of Rabbi Eliezer, from the *midrash Vayikra Rabbah*, while Rabbi Yishmael's opinion comes from the *midrash Toras Cohanim*; two separate sources. We see that Rashi quite purposefully sought out those *midrashim* that fit his purpose. Can you see why he chose just these two reasons here and not any of the others?

YOUR ANSWER:

UNDERSTANDING RASHI'S CHOICES

An Answer: If we analyze the two opinions given here we see that they both are based on, and have ties with, the immediate surrounding context of this verse. The first opinion, that of Rabbi Eliezer, is that they died because they decided a point of law on their own. Which law? that of bringing their own fire into the Tabernacle. This point is connected with the verse immediately before our verse. There it says "A fire went out from before *Hashem* and consumed [the offering on the altar]." Did you notice that our verse closely parallels that verse by saying "And a fire went out from before *Hashem* and consumed them..." Their bringing the fire without Moses' consent was their fatal mistake.

The second opinion, that of Rabbi Yishmael, is clearly based on the verse that comes after this incident, as Rashi says — the laws prohibiting imbibing alcoholic beverages before serving in the Tabernacle.

So Rashi has chosen just those *midrashim* that have an anchor in the context of our verse. On the other hand, the sins of the Golden Calf, of staring at G-d or the prohibition of entering the Holy of Holies are not mentioned here. Rashi thus does not draw on those other *midrashim* here to enlighten us as to Nadav and Avihu's sin.

CONFLICTING *MIDRASHIM*

Lest the student ask: But which is the truth? Which is the real reason for their deaths? He must understand that *midrash-aggadah* is not *midrash-halacha*. In the realm of *halacha* we can end up with only one final decisive conclusion. The world of *midrash-aggadah* is different. The *midrash* exists to teach us a lesson, either moral, ethical or religious. Many lessons can be learned from any one incident. So too in our case - many lessons can be learned from the tragic deaths of such righteous individuals as Nadav and Avihu. This is what the Sages are doing when they suggest the different sins of these men. And this, too, is what Rashi is doing when he cites them, albeit in different places and in different contexts.

LESSON

When Rashi cites a *midrash* which seems to contradict what the Torah itself has said, there is cause for reflection and deeper analysis. And when Rashi chooses a particular *midrash* from among many, he has a reason for doing so.

THE PARABLE

At the end of this comment, Rashi cites a parable about a king and the faithful member of his household. Then Rashi does a very strange thing, he leaves off without telling us the parable! One could ask: If the parable could be helpful in understanding the verse, why not quote the whole parable. And if it would not significantly enlighten us, why mention it at all? This is not the only instance of Rashi teasing us by quoting only the first few words of a parable without finishing it. Why?

This is not easy to understand. Shmuel Gelbard (author of *Liphshuto shel Rashi*) has suggested that Rashi did this intentionally in order to whet the student's appetite and entice him to look up the source for himself. In this way Rashi would encourage the student to become more independent in his learning. The student would open up the *midrash* and maybe find other things of interest. Rashi would then be acting as a true teacher, making himself dispensable, as the student explored new areas on his own.

Logical thinking is an indispensable aid to understanding Rashi.

Leviticus 10:4,5

4. וַיִּקְרָא מֹשֶׁה אֶל־מִישָׁאֵל וְאֶל אֶלְצָפָן בְּנֵי עֻזִּיאֵל דֹּד אַהֲרֹן וַיֹּאמֶר אֲלֵהֶם קִרְבוּ שְׂאוּ אֶת־אֲחֵיכֶם מֵאֵת פְּנֵי־הַקֹּדֶשׁ אֶל־מִחוּץ לַמַּחֲנֶה.

5. וַיִּקְרְבוּ וַיִּשָּׂאֻם בְּכֻתֳּנֹתָם אֶל־מִחוּץ לַמַּחֲנֶה כַּאֲשֶׁר דִּבֶּר מֹשֶׁה.

בכתנתם. שֶׁל מֵתִים. מְלַמֵּד שֶׁלֹּא נִשְׂרְפוּ בִּגְדֵיהֶם אֶלָּא נִשְׁמָתָם, כְּמִין שְׁנֵי חוּטִין שֶׁל אֵשׁ נִכְנְסוּ לְתוֹךְ חוֹטְמֵיהֶם.

With their robes: *Rashi:* [the robes] of the deceased. This teaches us that their garments were not burned only their souls; something like two threads of fire entered their nostrils.

What Is Rashi Saying?

Rashi is telling us that the robes referred to in our verse were the robes of Nadav and Avihu. Since it only says "their robes" it is not clear whose robes — either those of Mishael and Eltzafan, cousins of the deceased, who removed the dead bodies from the Tabernacle or the robes of the deceased themselves.

What would you ask here?

Remember a simple rule of thumb. When Rashi tells us something we apparently already know, we must ask: What's bothering Rashi? When he tells us something we didn't know previously, we ask: How does Rashi know this?

Your Question:

Questioning Rashi

A Question: How does Rashi know that these were the robes of Nadav and Avihu and not those of Mishael and Eltzafan?

Can you figure out what allowed Rashi to draw such a conclusion?

Your Answer:

Understanding Rashi

I will present two answers that are given to this question. Which of the two seems best to you?

> * An answer given here is that כתנות were one of the priestly garments and not the garb of the Levites. And since Mishael and Eltzafan were Levites and not priests, these robes must be those of the dead priests, Nadav and Avihu.

> * Another answer given is that if these were the robes of Mishael and Eltzafan there would be no point in the Torah mentioning it. It is an irrelevant piece of information.

Which answer seems best to you?

Why?

Your Choice:

Understanding Rashi's Thinking

An Answer: It seems to me that only the second answer reflects Rash's logical thinking style. First of all, the Levites almost certainly had their own robes even if they weren't the linen robes that the priests wore. They wore something, why not robes? So these could have been the non-priestly robes of Mishael and Eltzafan. But more to the point: If they were the robes of Mishael and Eltzafan, why are they mentioned at all? This would be an irrelevant fact. Rashi is always hyper sensitive to any extra words in the Torah and the need to explain them. In fact, all Torah commentary (including the Talmud) is based on this approach. The Torah does not tell us anything irrelevant to its message. To tell us that Mishael and Eltzafan dragged out the bodies while wearing their robes or with their robes, would be perhaps thorough reporting, but it would not enlighten us in any significant way. But if, on the other hand, these were the robes of the deceased, that meant that the fire that consumed Nadav and Avihu, didn't touch their clothing. Before the microwave, this was quite a feat! Thus, as Rashi continues, it teaches us the miraculous way Nadav and Avihu were killed by this Divine fire.

So only the second explanation for Rashi's comment gives a logically constructed answer. The kind that epitomizes Rashi style.

THE LESSON

When trying to understand Rashi's reason for one of his comments, think in terms of what is apparently redundant in the verse. What meaning might this redundancy carry? In this way we can get into Rashi's mental shoes and understand his way of thinking.

(See *Mesiach Ilmim*)

Leviticus 10:9

יַיִן וְשֵׁכָר אַל־תֵּשְׁתְּ אַתָּה וּבָנֶיךָ אִתָּךְ בְּבֹאֲכֶם אֶל־אֹהֶל מוֹעֵד וְלֹא תָמֻתוּ חֻקַּת עוֹלָם לְדֹרֹתֵיכֶם.

יין ושכר. יין דרך שכרותו.
Wine and intoxicating drink: *Rashi*: Wine in a manner that intoxicates.

WHAT IS RASHI SAYING?

Clearly Rashi changes the plain sense of the verse from "Wine *and* intoxicating drink" to "intoxicating wine."

YOUR QUESTION:

QUESTIONING RASHI

A Question: Why does Rashi do this? Why not accept the simple meaning "wine and intoxicating drink"?

What'a bothering Rashi?

YOUR ANSWER:

WHAT IS BOTHERING RASHI

An Answer: Simply put, wine is intoxicating and beer and liquor are also intoxicating drinks. Why, then, do we need both terms יין and שכר? The word שכר "intoxicating drink" would be sufficient because it also includes wine.

Rashi is wondering why the need for both terms.

How does his interpretation of these words deal with the problem?

YOUR ANSWER:

UNDERSTANDING RASHI

An Answer: The Torah is interested in having the priest do his holy service in a sober state. Thus the prohibition of wine is so that the priest will not become intoxicated. Rashi therefore sees the word שכר as describing the type (or amount) of wine that the Torah prohibits. "Wine that intoxicates" is prohibited, not grape juice.

Can you find an instance in the Torah where the word יין means a non-intoxicating grape drink?

YOUR ANSWER:

An Answer: When the Torah describes the Nazerite's vow (Numbers 6:3) it enumerates the drinks he is prohibited to partake of. Keep in mind that these all are derivatives of grapes. It says:

מִיַּיִן וְשֵׁכָר יַזִּיר חֹמֶץ יַיִן וְחֹמֶץ שֵׁכָר לֹא יִשְׁתֶּה וְכָל־מִשְׁרַת עֲנָבִים
לֹא יִשְׁתֶּה וַעֲנָבִים לַחִים וִיבֵשִׁים לֹא יֹאכֵל.

"From new or aged wine shall he abstain and he shall not drink vinegar of wine or vinegar of aged wine; anything in which grapes have been steeped he shall not drink, and fresh and dried grapes he shall not eat."

Clearly grapes are the prohibited food here. Yet the Torah uses both words יין ושכר. One of them must mean an intoxicating grape drink — שכר — the other not — יין. So we have יין which is non-intoxicating. However, in our verse which speaks of the priest serving in the Temple, the meaning of the word יין is restricted to intoxicating wine. That is what Rashi is teaching us.

A COMPARATIVE ANALYSIS

Rashi has shown us that two apparent nouns may really be a noun and the other a descriptive adjective.

Can you think of another instance in the Torah where Rashi does the same thing with two other nouns?

Your Answer:

An Answer: In Genesis 47:29 Jacob asks his son Joseph not to bury him in
Egypt. There he says:

וְעָשִׂיתָ עִמָּדִי חֶסֶד וֶאֱמֶת אַל־נָא תִקְבְּרֵנִי בְּמִצְרָיִם.

Rashi on that verse comments:

חסד ואמת. חסד שעושין עם המתים הוא חסד של אמת שאינו
מצפה לתשלום גמול.

Kindness and Truth: *Rashi:* Kindness that is done with
the dead is a **kindness of truth** for he does not expect to
receive any reward.

Here too Rashi takes these two words — חסד ואמת — not as two
separate nouns, but as a noun and an adjective. The Kindness (noun)
is described as one of Truth (adjective).

❖❖❖

*Rashi's sensitivity to the finer points of Biblical grammar are evident
and enlightening.*

Leviticus 10: 19

וַיְדַבֵּר אַהֲרֹן אֶל־מֹשֶׁה הֵן הַיּוֹם הִקְרִיבוּ אֶת־חַטָּאתָם וְאֶת־עֹלָתָם
לִפְנֵי ה' וַתִּקְרֶאנָה אֹתִי כָּאֵלֶּה וְאָכַלְתִּי חַטָּאת הַיּוֹם הַיִּיטַב בְּעֵינֵי ה'.

וְאָכַלְתִּי חַטָּאת. ו אם **אכלתי הייטב** וגו'.
Had I eaten the sin offering: *Rashi:* **And if I had eaten**
it, would it be good etc."

THE BACKGROUND TO THIS VERSE

On the day of the dedication of the Tabernacle, two of Aaron's sons died
tragically as they brought an unsolicited offering in the Tabernacle. Aaron,
their father, in mourning for them, was nevertheless to continue with the
service. But he had not eaten the Sin offering which was part of the
dedication ceremony. Moses berates him for not having done so and at
the same time tells him to go ahead and eat the offering. Our verse is
Aaron's rebuttal to his brother Moses. With that in mind, let us examine
the verse and Rashi's comment.

What Is Rashi Doing?

Rashi has added but one word to the words of the Torah, the word "if". Why does he do this?

Should we ask was is bothering him? I think not. Notice the style of this comment; it is a short comment, only one word is added, it is inserted between the Torah's words. This is what I have called a Type II comment. It usually is meant to dispel a misunderstanding. It is more appropriate to ask: What misunderstanding is possible here?

Your Answer:

A Possible Misunderstanding

An Answer: The word ואכלתי can have one of two meanings:

1: And I ate (here the letter ו is a connecting letter, meaning "and" while the verb remains in the past tense.)

2: I will eat (here the letter ו converts past to future.)

One might think that Aaron is arguing with Moses and saying "If I will eat the offering (as you suggest), would it be right in the eyes of G-d?" This would be choice #2 above.

Rashi chooses #1, leaving the verb in the past tense. But of course it cannot literally mean "I ate" because that's what the whole argument between Aaron and Moses is about — Why did Aaron *not* eat it. So Rashi makes one emendation by adding the word "If" as to say "If I had eaten it would that have been right?" See the verb remains in the past tense and it still makes sense within the context.

But you should not let Rashi off so easily. You should have a question to ask.

Your Question

Questioning Rashi

A Question: Maybe the correct reading is "And I will eat." In Biblical Hebrew this is a perfectly legitimate interpretation. How does Rashi know that choice # 1 is the correct one?

Your Answer:

EVIDENCE FOR RASHI'S CHOICE

An Answer: Rashi knows that the correct reading is past tense because of where the accent (musical note — 'trop') is located. Since it is placed under the letter ּכ, which is further back in the word, it must remain in the past tense. Were it to be converted to future tense then the accent would be at the end of the word, under the letter ּת. This is Rashi's reliable clue and this is what he comes to teach us here with his oh-so-brief comment.

The placing of the accent is crucial to a correct understanding of Hebrew. A common example is from the *Shema* recited daily.

וּקְשַׁרְתָּם לְאוֹת עַל־יָדֶךָ...

And you shall bind them...

וּכְתַבְתָּם עַל־מְזֻזוֹת בֵּיתֶךָ וּבִשְׁעָרֶיךָ.

And you shall write them ...

In each case, reading these words incorrectly with the accent at the beginning of the word would change its meaning to: "And you bound them" and "and you wrote them.." This is, of course, not the correct meaning.

In our verse, Rashi likewise, makes us aware of the significance of this subtle, often overlooked, grammatical nuance.

(See *Lashon Chaim*)

Rashi applies a midrash where it best serves his needs as commentator.

Leviticus 11:1,2

וַיְדַבֵּר הי אֶל־מֹשֶׁה וְאֶל־אַהֲרֹן לֵאמֹר אֲלֵהֶם.

דַּבְּרוּ אֶל־בְּנֵי יִשְׂרָאֵל לֵאמֹר זֹאת הַחַיָּה אֲשֶׁר תֹּאכְלוּ מִכָּל־הַבְּהֵמָה אֲשֶׁר עַל־הָאָרֶץ.

אל משה ואל אהרן. למשה אמר שיאמר לאהרן.

לאמר אליהם. אמר שיאמר לאלעזר ולאיתמר, או אינו אלא לאמר לישראל, כשהוא אומר: דברו אל בני ישראל, הרי דבור אמור לישראל, הא מה אני מקיים: לאמר אליהם? לבניו – לאלעזר ולאיתמר.

דברו אל בני ישראל. את כולם השוה להיות שלוחים בדבור זה, לפי שהושוו בדמימה וקבלו עליהם גזירת המקום מאהבה.

To Moses and to Aaron: *Rashi:* To Moses he said, to say to Aaron.

To say to them: *Rashi:* He said that he [Aaron] should tell this to Elazar and to Itamar. Or perhaps [you will assume this means] to say to Israel? But when it says "Speak to the Children of Israel" this refers to [telling] Israel. What then am I to make of "to say to them"? [It must mean] To his children, to Elazar and to Itamar.

Speak to the Children of Israel: *Rashi:* He (G-d) equated all of them (Moses, Aaron, Elazar and Itamar) to be His messengers for this command. Because they were all equal in remaining silent [after the deaths of Nadav and Avihu] and accepting this decree of G-d with love.

WHAT IS RASHI SAYING?

By means of a step-wise analysis, Rashi shows that the words "Speak to the Children of Israel" are addressed to all four people, Moses, Aaron, Elazar and Itamar. They are the ones told to speak to the Children of Israel. First Rashi shows that the word אליהם in the verse "And *Hashem* spoke to Moses and Aaron to say to *them*" (verse 11:1) means to Elazar and Itamar. While it could easily have been interpreted as meaning: to Moses and Aaron. But, then, this would be unnecessary, for the verse already says that *Hashem* was speaking to Moses and Aaron. In effect this means that G-d was commanding not just Moses and Aaron but also Elazar and Itamar to speak to the Children of Israel.

But this is quite unusual since Elazar and Itamar are never honored with the task of giving over G-d's commands to the people. Rashi gives us the reason for this unusual step: It is their reward for accepting with love the death of their brothers, Nadav and Avihu, just as Aaron their father had silently accepted this divine decree.

THE *MIDRASHIC* SOURCE

This explanation is from the *midrash* but, and this is what is puzzling, the *midrash* quotes it in conjunction with a previous verse (Lev. 10:12).

וַיְדַבֵּר מֹשֶׁה אֶל־אַהֲרֹן וְאֶל אֶלְעָזָר וְאֶל־אִיתָמָר בָּנָיו הַנּוֹתָרִים קְחוּ
אֶת־הַמִּנְחָה הַנּוֹתֶרֶת מֵאִשֵּׁי הי וְאִכְלוּהָ מַצּוֹת אֵצֶל הַמִּזְבֵּחַ כִּי קֹדֶשׁ
קָדָשִׁים הוּא.

It is on this verse that the *midrash* commented that all four people were equated, all equally commanded to bring the meal offering because of their loving acceptance of G-d's harsh decree.

At first glance, this verse seems a much more appropriate basis for this *midrash* than our verse, to which Rashi attaches it. It seems more appropriate for the following reasons:

* The four are explicitly mentioned in 10:12, while they are mentioned only by inference in our verse.

* The *midrash's* verse comes immediately after the deaths of Nadav and Avihu, when it would be appropriate to reward them for their silent acceptance of the tragedy.

Why then did Rashi transfer the *midrash* to our verse?

Can you justify this?

YOUR ANSWER:

UNDERSTANDING RASHI'S *MIDRASH* TRANSFER

Let us be aware of what Rashi has done. He has shown us, in his comment to the previous verse, by a logical analysis and the process of elimination, that the words דברו אל בני ישראל in our verse are addressed to Moses, Aaron and *also to Elazar and Itamar*. Rashi, as Torah commentator, now had to explain why Elazar and Itamar were, against all convention, included *here*. For this purpose he draws on the *midrash* that tells us of their special merit (*viz.* remaining silent in the wake of their brothers' tragic death). The fact that this *midrash* is applied to another purpose.

We can also understand why this reward is particularly appropriate here, even more so than it is in verse 10:12. Here *Hashem,* Himself, is speaking, there Moses was speaking. G-d's designation of Elazar and Itamar is an even more impressive expression of their worthiness than when Moses did it in verse 10:12. Furthermore, the privilege of speaking to the people was a more public act, and thus, more of an honor, than privately partaking of the meal offering (as in verse 10:12 above). Also, we can add, that there is an element of poetic justice in this reward. They remained silent and, as reward, were given the privilege to speak.

For all these reasons Rashi chose to transfer the *midrash* to our verse.

But, then, if everything is so logical, why did the Sages who compiled the *midrash* not do what Rashi did?

The answer is that the *midrash* and Rashi have different goals. The *midrash* wanted to point out the merit due Itamar and Elazar. It did so at the first opportunity, which was on verse 10:12. Rashi, on the other hand, is not a compiler of *midrash*, as he himself has said. He is a Torah commentator; in that capacity, he chose the verse in the Torah that needed to be explained; this was our verse 11:2. The *midrash* was his means of explaining it.

The Lesson

It is important to be aware, as we pointed out in our introduction, that Rashi and the *midrash* have different goals. Remembering this lesson is extremely helpful in better understanding Rashi's use of *midrash*.

(See *L'iphsuto shel Rashi*)

A classic example of a Type II comment. See how Rashi weaves his comment in between the Torah's words to clarify an ambiguity.

Leviticus 11:32

וְכֹל אֲשֶׁר־יִפֹּל עָלָיו מֵהֶם בְּמֹתָם יִטְמָא מִכָּל־כְּלִי־עֵץ אוֹ בֶגֶד אוֹ־עוֹר אוֹ שָׂק כָּל־כְּלִי אֲשֶׁר יֵעָשֶׂה מְלָאכָה בָּהֶם בַּמַּיִם יוּבָא וְטָמֵא עַד־הָעֶרֶב וְטָהֵר.

בַּמַּיִם יוּבָא. וְאַף לְאַחַר טְבִילָתוֹ **טָמֵא** הוּא לִתְרוּמָה **עַד הָעֶרֶב** וְאַחַר כָּךְ **וְטָהֵר** בְּהֶעֱרֵב הַשֶּׁמֶשׁ.

It must be brought into water: *Rashi:* **But** even after it has been immersed **it is unclean** in respect to *terumah* **until the evening and** then with the setting of the sun **it is clean.**

INTRODUCTORY NOTE

A brief note on the laws of ritual purity of objects may be helpful here. If one of the reptiles mentioned above (29,30) is dead and touches a wooden vessel or a leather or cloth garment, it makes that object ritually impure טמא. The vessel can be purified if is immersed in a *mikveh*. There are various levels of ritual purity: 1) Purity sufficient for daily activities; 2) Purity necessary for *terumah* (the tithing given the priest); 3) Purity necessary for the sacrificial food. These three levels require different levels of purification. Our verse deals with these levels.

WHAT IS RASHI DOING?

The words in bold print are the Torah's words, those in between are Rashi's addition. This is what I call a Type II comment.

Rashi's comment tells us that although the vessel was immersed in the *mikveh,* nevertheless, it has not yet achieved the higher levels of purity.

QUESTIONING RASHI

What kind of question would you ask on a Type II comment?

YOUR QUESTION:

WHAT MISUNDERSTANDING IS POSSIBLE HERE? _____

An Answer: This type of comment is meant to steer us away from a possible misunderstanding.

What might be misunderstood in this verse?

Look at the verse carefully.

YOUR ANSWER:

A MISUNDERSTANDING _____

An Answer: The verse says: "shall be brought into water and be unclean..." What does that mean?

Does bringing them into water (the *mikveh*) make them unclean!! That seems ridiculous, immersing in a *mikveh* doesn't make a person or a vessel ritually unclean! What, then, do the words "shall be brought into water and be unclean" mean?

Rashi's comment is directed at dispelling that misreading of the verse. He gives us the correct reading by his skillful addition of several well-placed words. Do you see what he does?

UNDERSTANDING RASHI _____

An Answer: While retaining each of the Torah's original words, Rashi inserts the missing, implied, meaning of the verse. Notice that Rashi separates the words "shall be brought into water" from "and be unclean." In this way he avoids the misreading of these words. Notice also a very subtle move that Rashi makes. He breaks up the word וטמא into two parts. First is the letter ו "and even" at the very beginning of this comment, then his additional words ("even after immersion") then the word טמא "unclean." We now see that the verse doesn't mean "shall be brought into water and be unclean." Rather **shall be brought into water** ...and even after this it remains ... **unclean** for the higher level of purity (*terumah*). This dispels the misunderstanding. Then Rashi inserts the words "and afterwards" between the Torah's words עד הערב "until sunset" and וטהר "then it is clean" in order to show us the progressive steps in purification, as it moves from immersion in a *mikveh* to sunset. Rashi's precision, conciseness and craftsmanship are here exemplified.

THE LESSON

Here we see what is often said, but rarely fully appreciated, that every word in Rashi's comment is significant. By separating the word וטמא into two parts — first the letter ו then the word טמא, his insertion -"and even after immersion" — dispels a possible misunderstanding.

When Rashi cites more than one verse to explain a word, we must under-stand why.

Leviticus 12:4

וּשְׁלֹשִׁים יוֹם וּשְׁלֹשֶׁת יָמִים תֵּשֵׁב בִּדְמֵי טָהֳרָה בְּכָל־קֹדֶשׁ לֹא־תִגָּע
וְאֶל־הַמִּקְדָּשׁ לֹא תָבֹא עַד־מְלֹאת יְמֵי טָהֳרָהּ.

תֵּשֵׁב. אין תשב אלא לשון עכבה. כמו "ותשבו בקדש" (דברים
א:מו) "וישב באלוני ממרא" (בראשית יג:יח).

And she shall abide. *Rashi*: The word תשב here means
non other than "to remain" ("to abide", "to stay") as in
"you stayed in Kaddaish" (Deut. 1:46) and "he stayed in
the Plains of Mamre" (Gen. 13:18).

Introduction to the Laws of a Woman after Childbirth

A few words of introduction are necessary here. According to the Torah,
a woman with a flow of blood is prohibited from having relations with
her husband and, in the time of the Temple, was prohibited from touch-
ing sacrificial food or entering the Temple. According to the Torah, a
menstruating woman was considered spiritually unclean (in the above
sense) for the period of time that she saw blood. Afterwards she was
considered spiritually pure. However, the laws of a woman after childbirth are different. For the first week after childbirth she may not be with
her husband; thereafter (for thirty-three days after the birth of a boy,
sixty-six days after the birth of a girl) she may be with her husband *even
if she continues to have a flow of blood*. These are called her "days of
purity" meaning that she is pure even if she sees blood. On the other
hand, paradoxically, during these thirty-three days she continues to be
forbidden to touch holy foods or enter the Temple, *even if she has no
flow of blood*.

With this in mind, let us look at Rashi's comment.

What Is Rashi Saying?

Rashi is telling us the meaning of a familiar and apparently simple word, תשב. Here the word does not have its usual meaning of "to sit," as in הוא ישב פתח האהל, "He was sitting at the entrance of the tent" (Gen. 18:1). Here it means "to remain." Rashi cites two verses as evidence that this can be the meaning of this word, one from Deuteronomy and the other from Genesis.

What would you ask here?

Your Question:

Questioning Rashi

Some Questions:

In what sense does the word תשב mean "to remain"? What is he clarifying here? What is not clear?

Another question is, why the need to cite two verses? He could have made his point just as well with only one verse.

What is Rashi Clarifying?

An Answer: Certainly the woman is not sitting in her "pure blood". That conjures up a very strange sight indeed! So she must be "remaining in her state of pure blood." In what sense is she "remaining"?

Hint: Read this verse carefully and make sense out it.

Your Answer:

Understanding Rashi

An Answer: This is a moot point. Taken on face value, the verse is not clear at all. It says:

"For thirty-three days she shall remain [in the status] of her pure blood. She shall not touch anything holy and she shall not come into the Temple until the completion of her days of purity."

Now we ask:

If her blood is "pure" why can't she go into the Temple? And if she is not pure, why is it called "her pure blood"?

Clearly we have two opposite and paradoxical situations. On the one hand: The woman becomes pure after a week and may be with her husband *even if she continues to have a blood flow*. On the other hand: The woman continues to be "impure" in that she is not allowed to enter the Temple for an additional thirty-three days *even if her blood flow ceases before that*.

With this in mind, we realize that Rashi is telling us that the woman "remains" pure (regarding her relationship with her husband) even if she sees blood. At the same time, she also "remains" impure (regarding entering the Temple) even if she does not see any blood.

A Deeper Look — Rashi's Quotes

Rashi cites two verses where the verb ישב means "to remain", and not "to dwell" or "to sit" which are the more common meanings. Let us examine these quotes and see what we discover.

We had asked: Why the need for two quotes when one would make the same point? These are not the only verses in the Torah where the word ישב means "to remain," so it is clear that Rashi has chosen these two for a purpose. Why?

Look at the verses.

1) The first is from Deuteronomy 1:46:

וַתֵּשְׁבוּ בְקָדֵשׁ יָמִים רַבִּים כַּיָּמִים אֲשֶׁר יְשַׁבְתֶּם.

The background to this verse is: Moses is recounting to the people the events after the sin of the Spies when they were condemned to remain in the wilderness another 38 years. Rashi quotes the verse in Deuteronomy to show that the word תשב can mean "to remain" (and not "to dwell"). The meaning being that although they were to have entered the Land of Israel immediately, they "remained" (were detained) in Kaddaish many days as a punishment.

2) The second verse comes from Genesis 13:18:

וַיֶּאֱהַל אַבְרָם וַיָּבֹא וַיֵּשֶׁב בְּאֵלֹנֵי מַמְרֵא אֲשֶׁר בְּחֶבְרוֹן וַיִּבֶן שָׁם מִזְבֵּחַ לַה׳.

The background to this verse is: G-d told Abram, after he had entered the Land of Canaan, that he is to travel the length and breadth of the land. The next verse is the one Rashi quotes.

With this in mind can you understand why Rashi cited these two verses to support his claim that ישב can mean "to remain"?

Your Answer:

A Deeper Understanding

An Answer: The Lubavitcher Rebbe, Rav Menachem Mendel Schneerson, זצ"ל, offers a brilliant insight into this Rashi. It illustrates Rashi's subtle thinking and the importance of taking every one of his quotes seriously.

Remember we had said that this verse has a paradoxical message. On the one hand, the woman, after childbirth, is "pure" even if she sees blood during the thirty three days she may, in fact, be with her husband. On the other hand, she is "impure" in that even if her blood flow ceases she may still not enter the Temple during these same thirty three days.

Rashi uses the word עכבה in two possible ways:

1) "to restrain."

2) "to remain."

The Jews in the wilderness were *restrained* from going into the Land of Canaan (see the verses Deut. 1:35ff). The woman is likewise *restrained* from going into the Temple, even though she has no blood flow. For this reason Rashi needed to cite the verse in Deutoronomy.

Abram, on the other hand, wasn't restrained. Just the opposite, he was told to travel the length and breadth of the Land, yet he *remained* in one place, the Plains of Mamre. Likewise, the woman *remains* in her state of "pure blood," (she is certainly not "restrained") and may be with her husband even though she has seen blood. To make this point, Rashi also needs the verse about Abram from Genesis.

Because Rashi was relating to these two different meanings of ישב in this one verse, he saw the need to cite two different verses, which translate this verb in a way that means either "to hold back" or "to be held back." Both these meanings are relevant in our unusual verse.

תָזְרִיעַ

The Lesson

Rashi's genius shines through, once we plumb the depth of his seemingly simple comment. Never take anything in his commentary for granted. Every quote deserves further probing.

(See *Biyurim L'pirush Rashi* of the Lubavitcher Rebbe)

Leviticus 12:8

וְאִם־לֹא תִמְצָא יָדָהּ דֵּי שֶׂה וְלָקְחָה שְׁתֵּי־תֹרִים אוֹ שְׁנֵי בְּנֵי יוֹנָה אֶחָד לְעֹלָה וְאֶחָד לְחַטָּאת וְכִפֶּר עָלֶיהָ הַכֹּהֵן וְטָהֵרָה.

אֶחָד לְעֹלָה וְאֶחָד לְחַטָּאת. לֹא הִקְדִּימָה הַכָּתוּב אֶלָּא לַמִּקְרָאָה אֲבָל לְהַקְרָבָה חַטַּאת קוֹדֶם לְעוֹלָה. כַּךְ שָׁנִינוּ בִּזְבָחִים בְּפֶרֶק כָּל הַתָּדִיר.

One as a burnt-offering and one as a sin-offering: *Rashi*: The verse only placed [the burnt-offering] first for the purpose of reading [in the Torah] but regarding offering it, the sin-offering precedes the burnt-offering. Thus we have learned in tractate *Zevachim* (90a) in the chapter *kol hatadir*.

What Is Rashi Saying?

The Torah tells us that a woman after childbirth is to bring two sacrificial offerings; a burnt offering and a sin offering. Rashi points out that the order of the sacrifices as listed in this verse, the burnt offering before the sin offering, is not the order that they are, in fact, to be offered in the Temple.

Your question:

Questioning Rashi

A Question: How does Rashi know that the order here is not followed when these birds are sacrificed ?

Actually, to be fair to the student, we should point out that Rashi himself tells us that this is learned from the Talmud in *Zevachim* 90a. So the surest way of understanding this comment is to see what the Sages say in *Zevachim*.

Understanding Rashi

Answer: The Sages cite verses in *parashas Vayikra* ch. 5:7-9, where the Torah speaks of the guilt-offering (a type of sin-offering). It says:

> "....and he shall bring...two doves or two pigeons for *Hashem*, one for a sin-offering and one for a burnt-offering. And he shall bring them to the priest and he should sacrifice *the sin-offering first....and the second should be made a burnt-offering*, and the priest shall atone for him from his sin which he sinned, and he shall be forgiven."

We see clearly that the sin-offering is brought first, then the burnt-offering. The Sages learn that this order is to be followed whenever there are two offerings. This, then, is the source of Rashi's conclusion.

But we should still question this procedure.

Your question:

Questioning the Sages' Conclusion

A Question: Why is it necessary that the sin-offering be brought first?

Another Question:

If the sin-offering is first, why is the order in the Torah reversed?

Hint: Rashi himself deals with the first question in Leviticus 5:8.

Your Answer:

Understanding the Sages' Lesson

Answer: Rashi, on his commentary to Leviticus 5:8 writes:

> "The sin offering precedes the burnt-offering. To what can this be compared? To an advocate who entered [the palace] to obtain pardon for his client. [Once] the advocate gains pardon (with the sin-offering), the gift (burnt-offering) is brought afterwards."

The point being that atonement must first be made by means of the sin-offering, then, and only then, is it appropriate to give the gift, i.e., the burnt-offering. Giving the gift first would smack of bribery!

But the question remains: Why, then, does the Torah in our verse place the gift, the burnt-offering, before the sin-offering if that is not the order in which they are brought?

Can you think of a reason?

YOUR ANSWER:

A DEEPER UNDERSTANDING

A Possible Answer:

> The question must be asked: Why does a woman after childbirth have to bring a sin-offering at all? What sin has she committed? The Sages (tractate *Nida* 31b) explain that the reason for this offering is that while experiencing the painful birth pangs the woman may have sworn off any further relations with her husband, to prevent becoming pregnant again and having to go through the traumatic childbirth experience. Thus we see that in fact the woman did not sin in any "sinful" way. In her duress she uttered an oath, which she certainly didn't fully intend.
>
> In view of this, I would suggest that perhaps the Torah mentioned the sin-offering last, after the burnt-offering, in order to de-emphasize its significance in this unusual case. Nevertheless, in actual practice the woman must first bring her sin-offering before her gift offering, for the reason stated above.

A Rashi-comment that deals with grammar, something Rashi does frequently in his commentary. But here there is a catch.

Leviticus 13:8

וְרָאָה הַכֹּהֵן וְהִנֵּה פָּשְׂתָה הַמִּסְפַּחַת בָּעוֹר וְטִמְּאוֹ הַכֹּהֵן צָרַעַת הִוא.

צרעת הוא. המספחת הזאת. **צרעת.** לשון נקבה. **נגע.** לשון זכר.
It is tzora'as. *Rashi:* This *mispachas.* **Tzora'as:** *Rashi:*
(this noun) is feminine gender. **Nega:** *Rashi:* (this noun)
is masculine gender.

Aside from the grammatical lesson, what would you ask here?

Hint: Look at the verse and at Rashi.

YOUR QUESTION:

QUESTIONING RASHI

A Question: Rashi gives us the genders of two words, צרעת and נגע, but the
word נגע does not appear in this verse!

Why do you think he does this?

Note: This Rashi has bothered many commentaries.

YOUR ANSWER:

WHAT IS BOTHERING RASHI?

An Answer: This chapter 13 is replete with a confusing array of masculine/
feminine pronouns. It is not always easy to make out what the pronouns היא (feminine) and הוא (masculine) refer to. Rashi makes
his comment here because until now the subject has been the word
נגע and has been treated as a masculine noun. See, for example,
verse 13:5, which says:

וְהִנֵּה הַנֶּגַע עָמַד בְּעֵינָיו וגו'

"And behold, the affliction retained *its* (masculine) color etc."

On the other hand, the upcoming verse (13:9) says:

נֶגַע צָרַעַת כִּי תִהְיֶה בְּאָדָם וגו'

"An affliction of *tzora'as* when *it* (feminine) will be in a person
etc."

This confusion is likely what was bothering Rashi.

Understanding Rashi

Therefore, Rashi saw the need to correct a possible misunderstanding at this point in his commentary by instructing us as to the gender status of the two basic words here: נגע and צרעת. The verse coming up has the combination term נגע צרעת and the verb which follows (תהיה) is in the feminine form. Rashi's comment makes it clear that the feminine gender is appropriate here because the main word in the combined term נגע צרעת is צרעת and therefore is feminine.

A Deeper Look

Nevertheless, the confusion is especially pronounced when we look at the combined term נגע צורעת, "an affliction of *tzora'as*," as it appears in different contexts in this chapter.

Sometimes this term is considered masculine (see 13:3) and sometimes feminine (see 13:20). Below is a list of the various verses where this combined term is used in this chapter. Review the list. Can you find any method to the masculine/feminine gender question? Why is it treated sometimes as a masculine term and sometimes as a feminine term?

1. ויקרא יג:ג: וְרָאָה הַכֹּהֵן אֶת־הַנֶּגַע בְּעוֹר הַבָּשָׂר וְשֵׂעָר בַּנֶּגַע הָפַךְ לָבָן וּמַרְאֵה הַנֶּגַע עָמֹק מֵעוֹר בְּשָׂרוֹ **נֶגַע צָרַעַת הוּא** וְרָאָהוּ הַכֹּהֵן וְטִמֵּא אֹתוֹ.

2. יג:ט: נֶגַע צָרַעַת כִּי תִהְיֶה בְּאָדָם וְהוּבָא אֶל־הַכֹּהֵן.

3. יג:כב: וְרָאָה הַכֹּהֵן וְהִנֵּה מַרְאֶהָ שָׁפָל מִן־הָעוֹר וּשְׂעָרָהּ הָפַךְ לָבָן וְטִמְּאוֹ הַכֹּהֵן **נֶגַע־צָרַעַת הוּא** (הִיא) בַּשְּׁחִין פָּרָחָה.

4. יג:כה: וְרָאָה אֹתָהּ הַכֹּהֵן וְהִנֵּה נֶהְפַּךְ שֵׂעָר לָבָן בַּבַּהֶרֶת וּמַרְאֶהָ עָמֹק מִן־הָעוֹר **צָרַעַת הוּא** (הִיא) בַּמִּכְוָה פָּרָחָה וְטִמֵּא אֹתוֹ הַכֹּהֵן **נֶגַע צָרַעַת הוּא** (הִיא).

5. יג:כז: וְרָאָהוּ הַכֹּהֵן בַּיּוֹם הַשְּׁבִיעִי אִם־פָּשֹׂה תִפְשֶׂה בָּעוֹר וְטִמֵּא הַכֹּהֵן אֹתוֹ **נֶגַע צָרַעַת הוּא** (הִיא).

6. יג:מז: וְהַבֶּגֶד כִּי־יִהְיֶה בוֹ נֶגַע צָרָעַת בְּבֶגֶד צֶמֶר אוֹ בְּבֶגֶד פִּשְׁתִּים.

7. יג:מט: וְהָיָה הַנֶּגַע יְרַקְרַק אוֹ אֲדַמְדָּם בַּבֶּגֶד אוֹ בָעוֹר אוֹ־בַשְּׁתִי אוֹ־בָעֵרֶב אוֹ בְכָל־כְּלִי־עוֹר **נֶגַע צָרַעַת הוּא** וְהָרְאָה אֶת הַכֹּהֵן.

Note that verses 1, 6 and 7 use the masculine, while verses 2, 3, 4 and 5 use the feminine.

Do you find any consistency here?

YOUR ANSWER:

UNDERSTANDING THE TORAH'S GRAMMAR

An Answer: If you check each of the verses above you will see that the gender is not determined by the words נגע צרעת, but rather by the subject of the particular law discussed. Take, for example,

Leviticus 13:19,20:

19. וְהָיָה בִּמְקוֹם הַשְּׁחִין שְׂאֵת לְבָנָה אוֹ בַהֶרֶת לְבָנָה אֲדַמְדָּמֶת וְנִרְאָה אֶל־הַכֹּהֵן.

20. וְרָאָה הַכֹּהֵן וְהִנֵּה מַרְאֶהָ שָׁפָל מִן־הָעוֹר וּשְׂעָרָהּ הָפַךְ לָבָן וְטִמְּאוֹ הַכֹּהֵן נֶגַע־צָרַעַת הִוא (הִיא) בַּשְּׁחִין פָּרָחָה.

"And on the place of the inflammation there will be white rising or a white bright spot, streaked with red; it shall be shown to the priest. The priest shall look and behold, its appearance is lower than the skin and its hair has turned white. The priest shall declare him impure — it is an affliction of *tzora'as* that has erupted on the inflammation."

You can see that the subject of verse 20 is found in the previous verse, it is שאת לבנה או בהרת לבנה which are feminine terms. Therefore, when the Torah says נגע צרעת היא, it uses the feminine because it refers back to the words שאת או בהרת.

You will find this to be the explanation for each of the cases above. The combined term נגע צרעת is not the subject; rather, the subject is the particular affliction that is the focus of the law mentioned in the verse, which may be in either the masculine or feminine gender.

A very brief comment. Understanding it fully makes us aware of an unclarity in the text not usually noticed.

Leviticus 13:12

וְאִם־פָּרוֹחַ תִּפְרַח הַצָּרַעַת בָּעוֹר וְכִסְּתָה הַצָּרַעַת אֵת כָּל־עוֹר הַנֶּגַע מֵרֹאשׁוֹ וְעַד־רַגְלָיו לְכָל־מַרְאֵה עֵינֵי הַכֹּהֵן.

מֵרֹאשׁוֹ. שֶׁל אדם וְעַד רַגְלָיו.

From his head: *Rashi:* of the man **unto his feet**.

What Is Rashi Saying?

The Hebrew word ראשו can mean either "his head" or "its head." The Torah says מראשו ועד רגליו which means either "from his head unto his feet" or "from its head unto its feet." Rashi tells us that the "leprosy covers all the man's skin from *his* head unto *his* feet."

Questioning Rashi

This is one of those brief (Type II) comments which Rashi inserts within the words of the Torah. These are meant to help us avoid a misunderstanding. Which misunderstanding is Rashi helping us avoid here?

Hint: Look closely at the entire verse. Translate it to yourself so that you understand it fully.

Your Answer:

A Possible Misunderstanding

Some English translations of the Torah incorrectly translate our verse as follows:

"If the leprosy will erupt on the skin and the leprosy will cover the entire skin of the affliction from his head to his feet, wherever the eyes of the priest can see."

Does this make sense to you? If you think it does, we'll ask:

What do these word mean: "leprosy will cover the entire skin of the affliction ..." How can the leprosy *cover* the affliction? The "affliction" and the "leprosy" are the exact same thing. They both refer to the same area of the skin that is affected/afflicted. If so, how can the leprosy cover *any less* than the entire skin of the affliction? The "cover" is the leprosy and the leprosy is the affliction.

So what, then, do these words mean?

YOUR ANSWER:

UNDERSTANDING RASHI

An Answer: According to Rashi, the Hebrew phrase וכסתה הצרעת את כל עור הנגע מראשו ועד רגליו is to be translated as follows: "and the leprosy covers all the skin of *him who has* the affliction from his head to his feet..." The words in italics are to be added. This is to say that the Hebrew word נגע does not mean "affliction," rather it means "the person who has the affliction."

If that is the case, then Rashi's comment is precise. He tells us that the words mean "From the head of the man (with the affliction) to his feet." Rashi intends to guard us against the possible misunderstanding that these words might mean "from the head (top) of the affliction to its feet (bottom)." Rather, the correct meaning is that this affliction (the leprosy) covers all the skin of the body of the afflicted person.

Can you find support for this interpretation which translates נגע as "the person with the affliction" and not just as "affliction" alone?

Hint: Look at other verses in this section.

YOUR ANSWER:

EVIDENCE FOR THIS INTERPRETATION

An Answer: See the very next verse, where we see that all the skin of the person is covered. "Then the priest shall see and behold the leprosy has covered **all his flesh**; he shall pronounce *him* clean *that has the* affliction. It is all turned white, he is clean." Likewise a previous verse (13:4) says "And if the bright spot...then the priest shall shut up (*he that has*) the affliction seven days." Here too the word נגע must mean the person who has the affliction and not just the affliction itself. The priest doesn't shut up "the affliction" without the person! The meaning is clearly that he "shuts up the person who has the affliction."

A Moral Lesson

We see from all this that the Torah equates the affliction, נגע, with the person who has the affliction. This is quite unusual, and the Torah may have done so to teach us something.

In the next chapter (Leviticus 14:4), Rashi tells us that the plague of leprosy comes upon a person as punishment for the sin of slander, לשון הרע. We also know that Miriam, after she spoke against her brother Moses, was stricken with leprosy (See Numbers 12:1 ff.). Several explanations have been offered as to why this punishment is meted out for this crime. Be that as it may, leprosy — נגעים — is the punishment for slander.

A person commits לשון הרע when he points out an actual fault of another person and implies that this one fault indicates that his whole character is blemished. This is called "character assassination." The victim's whole character is attacked. One fault is incorrectly assumed to equal the whole personality. How fitting, then, that the Torah, in its characteristically subtle way, should also equate the נגע with the whole person afflicted with the affliction! We have here an educational type of poetic justice, teaching us the insidiously destructive effects of slander.

Punishment, measure for measure.

Leviticus 13:46

כָּל־יְמֵי אֲשֶׁר הַנֶּגַע בּוֹ יִטְמָא טָמֵא הוּא בָּדָד יֵשֵׁב מִחוּץ לַמַּחֲנֶה מוֹשָׁבוֹ.

בָּדָד יֵשֵׁב. שֶׁלֹּא יִהְיוּ טְמֵאִים יוֹשְׁבִין עִמּוֹ. וְאָמְרוּ רַבּוֹתֵינוּ מַה נִּשְׁתַּנָּה מִשְּׁאָר טְמֵאִים לֵישֵׁב בָּדָד? הוֹאִיל וְהוּא הִבְדִּיל בִּלְשׁוֹן הָרַע בֵּין אִישׁ לְאִשְׁתּוֹ וּבֵין אִישׁ לְרֵעֵהוּ אַף הוּא יִבָּדֵל.

He shall abide alone. *Rashi*: (This means that) other unclean individuals shall not be with him. Our Rabbis have said: Why is he (the unclean leper) treated differently from other unclean people, that he should abide alone? Since he, with his slander, separated man from his wife or a man from his friend, he too must be separated (from everyone).

What would you ask here?

Your Question:

Questioning Rashi

A Question: Remember the rule: Whenever Rashi tells us something that we don't see in the Torah's words themselves, we ask:

How does Rashi know this? Or,

What's bothering Rashi that lead him to this conclusion?

Hint: Look carefully at the verse.

Your Answer:

What Is Bothering Rashi?

An Answer: The verse says: "He shall abide alone, outside the camp shall be his dwelling." If he is outside the camp, he is already alone! The word "alone" is unnecessary.

How does Rashi's comment deal with this?

Your Answer:

Understanding Rashi

An Answer: By adding the word "alone", the Torah tells us that he is outside the camp *and* also alone. That is, he is kept at a distance even from others who are also impure, for example, one impure due to having come in contact with a dead person. The slanderer is to be seperated even from these outside-the-camp people. However, the question whether he should be separated from other slanderers, as well, is one discussed and debated by the commentators. Logic would say that they should certainly be separated from one another. But, on the other hand, maybe living for awhile in a "slanderers' colony" would give these sinners a taste of their own medicine!

(See Talmud *Erechin* 16b)

A comment that has aroused much probing. Understanding it reveals how Rashi makes use of midrash in his commentary.

Leviticus 14: 4

וְצִוָּה הַכֹּהֵן וְלָקַח לַמִּטַּהֵר שְׁתֵּי־צִפֳּרִים חַיּוֹת טְהֹרוֹת וְעֵץ אֶרֶז וּשְׁנִי תוֹלַעַת וְאֵזֹב.

טהרות. פרט לעוף טמא, לפי שהנגעים באין על לשון הרע שהוא מעשה פטפוטי דברים לפיכך הוזקקו לטהרתו צפרים שמפטפטין תמיד בצפצוף קול.

Pure [birds]: *Rashi:* Excluding an impure (non-kosher) fowl. Because the afflictions come (as a punishment) for *lashon hara* (slander) which is an act of chattering, therefore birds are compulsory for purification because they chatter endlessly with a twittering (צפצוף) sound.

WHAT IS RASHI SAYING?

This comment has two parts to it. The first part tells us a basic law regarding the type of bird that may not be brought as a sacrifice for the leper. The second part tells the symbolic message of this offering.

What would you ask?

YOUR QUESTION:

QUESTIONING RASHI

A Question: Considering that Rashi brings both of the comments within one *dibbur hamaschil*, and seems to connect them, we would ask:

Why does he do this? Is there any connection between them?

To answer this question, we must first look at Rashi's sources and see how he uses them. Only then can we try to understand the inner meaning of his comment.

Rashi's *Midrashic* Sources

Rashi derives his comment from two different Rabbinical sources. The first is from *Toras Cohanim* which teaches us the halacha that impure birds are invalid for this offering. The second comes from the Talmud, *Erechin* 16b, which make the connection between "birds" who chatter and people who chatter with their slander. Let us look at what it says in *Toras Cohanim* and compare this with Rash's words.

טהורות: ולא טמאות

Pure [birds]: but not impure [birds].

Do you see any difference between Rashi's source and what Rashi himself says?

What difference can you point out?

Differences between Rashi and the *Midrash*

An Answer: One difference is that Rashi uses the singular עוף טמא while the *midrash* uses the plural ולא טמאות. While the commentaries discuss this switch, I don't think it is particularly significant because, as Rashi himself has said, singular nouns can be used for the plural, in the sense of a collective noun (see Genesis 32:6).

But there is another difference which may be more significant. Do you see it?

Another Difference:

Rashi says "an impure *fowl*" (עוף) while the verse says "*birds*" צפרים. Why does Rashi make this change?

This cannot be understood without some background information. The Talmud says (*Chulin* 139b) that the word צפור, as used in the Torah, always means a pure (kosher) bird, while the word עוף can mean either a pure or impure bird. Now, with this in mind, maybe you can come up with an explanation for Rashi's use of "fowl" instead of "bird."

To understand this comment you must be prepared to engage in some logical analysis.

Your Answer:

Understanding Rashi

An Answer: Rashi, seeing the comment in *Toras Cohanim*, understood that the opinion which excluded "impure" birds did not agree with the Talmudic opinion that the term "bird" means only "pure" birds. You see, since in the Talmudic opinion the word "birds" in the Torah can *only* mean "pure" birds, there is no need to exclude "impure" birds. But, on the other hand, according to the *Toras Cohanim*, the term "birds" may mean either pure or impure birds, therefore, it was necessary for the Torah to emphasize "pure birds" in order to exclude impure birds.

However, Rashi himself agrees with the Talmudic view that the term צפרים only means pure birds. But if this is so, then the Torah's wording "pure birds" is redundant, since all birds are pure. Rashi therefore intentionally used the term "fowl" (which is also a category of bird) to teach us that the word "pure" טהורות in the Torah is meant to exclude impure *fowls*.

But if you think about this more deeply you may have a question about the Torah's wording.

Your Question:

A Deeper Look

A Question: If Rashi used the word עוף why did the Torah use the word צפור? You understand that this is a problem for Rashi but not for the *midrash*. Because as we said the *midrashic* opinion is that "bird" may be either pure or impure. But since Rashi believes the term "bird" can only mean pure birds, therefore if the Torah is excluding an impure creature it should use the term "fowl" and not "bird."

Can you think of an answer why, in spite of this logic, the Torah used the word "birds" צפרים?

Your Answer:

A Deeper Understanding

An Answer: It is precisely for this reason that Rashi adds the second part of his comment. He makes the point that the Torah uses the word "birds" because they are an appropriate expiation for the sin of slander, the chattering of people being similar to the chattering of birds. It is for this reason that the Torah uses the term צפרים instead of fowl עוף, to drive home the ethical message.

We now see the inherent connection between the two parts of Rashi's comment. The recognition that the word "pure" excludes impure fowls (but not "birds") leads us to rethink the "inappropriateness" of the word צפור, why would the Torah use that word when it means "fowl"? This in turn leads us to understand why the Torah went out of its way to use the word צפרים in order to convey the symbolic significance of birds as an atonement for the slanderer.

RASHI'S CREATIVE USE OF MIDRASH

We see clearly how Rashi drew on several *midrashic* sources and blended them in an original way. What looked like an arbitrary association of ideas, turns out, after analysis of Rashi's thinking, to be a smooth-flowing line of reasoning.

(See *Levush Ha'orah*)

Sensitivity to an unusual word usage reveals a hidden treasure.

Leviticus 14:34

כִּי תָבֹאוּ אֶל־אֶרֶץ כְּנַעַן אֲשֶׁר אֲנִי נֹתֵן לָכֶם לַאֲחֻזָּה וְנָתַתִּי נֶגַע צָרַעַת בְּבֵית אֶרֶץ אֲחֻזַּתְכֶם.

וְנָתַתִּי נֶגַע צָרַעַת. בְּשׂוֹרָה הִיא לָהֶם שֶׁהַנְּגָעִים בָּאִים עֲלֵיהֶם, לְפִי שֶׁהִטְמִינוּ אֱמוֹרִיִּים מַטְמוֹנִיּוֹת שֶׁל זָהָב בְּקִירוֹת בָּתֵּיהֶם כָּל אַרְבָּעִים שָׁנָה שֶׁהָיוּ יִשְׂרָאֵל בַּמִּדְבָּר וְעַל יְדֵי הַנֶּגַע נוֹתֵץ הַבַּיִת וּמוֹצְאָן.

And I shall put the affliction of leprosy: *Rashi*: This is a good tiding for them, that the afflictions will come upon them. Because the Amorites hid treasures of gold in the walls of their homes during the whole forty years that Israel was in the desert; thus as a result of the affliction, he tears down his house and will find them.

The question on this comment should be obvious.

YOUR QUESTION:

QUESTIONING RASHI

A Question: Why does Rashi turn a plague into a good tiding!? Leprosy is certainly no blessing; on what basis does he see this plague as a positive message?

> *Hint:* Compare our verse with other verses above that tell of other plagues.
> Some examples: 13:2; 13:9; 13:29; 13:42; 13:47.

> What's bothering Rashi?

YOUR ANSWER:

WHAT IS BOTHERING RASHI?

An Answer: A comparison of our verse with other similar verses shows the
remarkable fact that only in our verse does the Torah use the word
ונתתי "and I will give" when referring to the onset of a plague. For
example, we find the verse dealing with an affliction on the head
of a person: "A man or a woman in whom there will be (יהיה) an
affliction etc." (Leviticus 13:29). It does not say "I will give an
affliction". Our verse is the only one in this chapter that uses the
word "give". We should also note that the word נתן has a positive
connotation. The word is similar to the Hebrew for gift — מתנה.

> Rashi is wondering why the Torah would choose such a word when it
> speaks of inflicting an affliction on the Israelite houses? How does his
> comment deal with the question?

YOUR ANSWER:

UNDERSTANDING RASHI

An Answer: Rashi (on the basis of a *midrash*) supplies the missing link, between affliction and blessing. The Canaanites (Amorites) who lived
in the Land before the Israelites conquered it, preserved their treasures in the walls of their homes. They did so because they had
heard of the Israelites' escape from Egypt and the miraculous split-
ting of the Reed Sea. They also must have heard of the Israelites'

intended destination, their own Land of Canaan. They were preparing for the eventual war of conquest by trying to preserve their
valuables from the invading army. *Hashem*, wanting to give the
Israelites a gift, taught them the laws of house-afflictions and the
need to tear down the walls. The Israelite owner would cure a plague
on his house by tearing down its walls and invariably discover the
hidden treasures.

See how this *drash* fits in so well with a future promise of *Hashem*. In
Deut. 6:10ff it says:

> "It shall be when *Hashem* your G-d **brings you to the Land** that
> *Hashem* swore to your forefathers to Abraham, to Isaac and to
> Jacob, **to give you** great and good cities that you did not build.
> **Houses filled with every good thing** that you did not fill..."

Notice the similarity between these words and the words in our verse.

Hashem's promise	The house-plague (our verse)
כי תבואו אל ארץ כנען	והיה כי יביאך אל הארץ
אֲשר אני נותן לכם	אשר נשבע...לתת לך
ונתתי נגע צרעת בבית ארץ אחזתכם	ובתים מלאים כל טוב

The above words make it clear that the plague of leprosy in the walls of
their newly acquired homes in Canaan would be a fulfillment of this
promise. The similarity between G-d's promise as recorded in
Deuteronomy and the wording in our verses is too great to be mere coincidence.

(See *Mizrachi*)

Rashi finds a hidden moral message.

Leviticus 14:35

וּבָא אֲשֶׁר־לוֹ הַבַּיִת וְהִגִּיד לַכֹּהֵן לֵאמֹר כְּנֶגַע נִרְאָה לִי בַּבָּיִת.

כנגע נראה לי בבית. שאפילו הוא תלמיד חכם ויודע שהוא נגע ודאי לא יפסוק דבר ברור לומר "נגע נראה לי" אלא "כנגע נראה לי."

Like an affliction has appeared to me in the house: *Rashi*: Even if he is a learned man who knows that it is definitely an affliction, he should not decide the matter definitively saying: "an affliction appeared to me" rather [he should say] "*like* an affliction appeared to me."

Rashi derives his comment from the mishna in *Negaim* 12:5. The basis for this idea is clear enough, since the Torah says כנגע נראה לי "like an affliction" and not just נגע נראה לי "an affliction", the mishna derives this lesson. In short, this is what was bothering the mishna and, in turn, what was bothering Rashi.

Questioning Rashi

But what is the significance of this lesson? Why shouldn't a person say with certainty, "I saw an affliction in my house" ?

Can you suggest an answer?

Your Answer:

Understanding Rashi

Some Answers:

Actually several answers have been suggested. Among them:

* It is not the layman's (the homeowner's) responsibility or prerogative, to declare a spot in his home to be officially "an affliction" of the halachic type, with all the halachic implications that follow (e.g. the vessels in the home becoming impure). This is the priest's job.

* It is factually incorrect for the home owner to declare this spot to be a נגע, only the priest can do this. Thus, for the home owner to make this statement would, in effect, be a lie (*Gur Aryeh*). One

must always distance oneself from saying untruths, in whatever circumstance.

* The man's definitive statement smacks of conceit. As if this man knows for certain that this spot is an halachically bona fide נגע. One should always be cautious and modest in one's declarations. As the Sages tell us (Tractate *Berochos* 4a):

למד לשונך לומר "איני יודע."

Teach your tongue to say, I don't know.

I would say that Rashi's point is the last one mentioned. When we consider that one of Rashi's purposes in his Torah commentary is to teach the student Torah and *derech eretz* (proper conduct) and remembering that he himself conducted himself faithfully according to this dictum (many times in his Torah commentary he declares "I don't know what this teaches us."), it is reasonable to assume that this is his message to us here.

A Closer Look

One Last Question:

> Why does Rashi (and the *mishna*) say "Even a learned man..." On what basis does he conclude that we are talking about a *Talmid Chacham*?

Your Answer:

An Answer: Remember, we are talking about a situation where a man found a strange spot on the walls of his home. A spot is a spot, as a rose is a rose, it may be greenish, it may be reddish, it may be any color. An ordinary person would call a home repair person to take care of mold in his home. Who would think that maybe this spot is a נגע, an affliction of the "house-leprosy" type ? Only a *Talmid Chacham*!

A Deeper Look

> Can you think of a reason why only in the case of the *tzora'as* of the house, and not in the cases of leprosy of a person or his garment, does the Torah say that the man reports to the priest "Like an affliction appeared to me..."?

Your Answer:

A Deeper Understanding

An Answer: In all the cases except that of the *tzora'as* of a house, the sufferer
goes personally to the priest. He needn't report anything, he shows
the priest the affliction on his body or his garment. But in the case
of an affliction found on the walls of a house — it would be a bit
difficult to transport the walls to the priest. So, here and only here,
the man first reports to the priest what he saw on the walls of his
house and then the priest makes a house call to declare the spot
pure or impure as the case may be.

(See *Mizrachi, Tosephos Yom Tov*)

A simple Type II comment with surprising supportive corroboration.

Leviticus 14:41

וְאֶת־הַבַּיִת יַקְצִעַ מִבַּיִת סָבִיב וְשָׁפְכוּ אֶת־הֶעָפָר אֲשֶׁר הִקְצוּ אֶל־
מִחוּץ לָעִיר אֶל־מָקוֹם טָמֵא.

מבית: מבפנים.

From "bayis": *Rashi*: on the inside.

Introductory Note

The laws regarding a leprous spot found on the walls of a house are
described in this section. For our purpose it is sufficient to say that if the
priest proclaims the spot to be *tzara'as* then the stones and the plaster
must be removed. The stones are taken down and the plaster is scraped
off the surrounding area.

Questioning Rashi

This is a short comment, very short. What has Rashi told us? Or, as with
many short comments which are of the Type II style, we would ask:
What misunderstanding is he helping us avoid?

Your Answer:

What Misunderstanding?

An Answer: We must see the Hebrew words to understand this comment. The verse says ואת הבית יקצע מבית סביב. The problem here is that the word בית is used twice in this verse but with different meanings. The word בית ordinarily means "house". But if we translated both words as "house", the verse would read: "And you should scrape the house from the house around about..." which could be interpreted to mean that one scrapes the whole house round about. This is incorrect; one needn't scrape the plaster off the whole house.

Rashi wants to help us avoid this misunderstanding.

How does Rashi's comment help us?

Your Answer:

Understanding Rashi

Rashi tells us that the word מבית has another, less common, meaning; it means "inside." He is saying that this is the meaning of the word בית the second time it appears in our verse. The meaning, therefore, is: "He should scrape the house inside around..."

The purpose and the meaning of Rashi's comment are evident, viz,. to show us the correct meaning of this word and to differentiate it from the similar word בית.

Questioning Deeper

But for a fuller understanding, we should ask another question.

How does Rashi know that, in fact, this is the correct meaning here?

Can you find evidence for this, either in this *parasha* or elsewhere in the Torah?

Your Answer:

A Deeper Understanding

An Answer: The word מבית is used elsewhere in the Torah and there it clearly means "on the inside". In the story of Noah, when the ark is described (Genesis 6:14), it says :

וְכָפַרְתָּ אֹתָהּ מִבַּיִת וּמִחוּץ בַּכֹּפֶר.

...and you shall tar it inside and out with pitch.

So we see this word means "inside."

But can you also find some additional evidence that the word מבית here does not mean "from the house"?

Hint: In this *parasha* itself.

YOUR ANSWER:

An Answer: Throughout this section the word בית always has a ה before it, meaning "the house". This is so in every one of the 28 times the word appears. But our word is not מהבית which would mean "from **the** house." Our word is מבית, it thus has a different meaning — "from inside."

(See *Mizrachi*)

SURPRISING SUPPORTIVE EVIDENCE

Now we come to something which I think is quite interesting. You may or may not know that the Torah has its own pattern of writing. Not only *what* the Torah says must be analyzed, but also *how* it says *what* it says, also requires analysis. One of the fascinating characteristics of Torah writing is the Seven Code. This means that central theme words are often repeated seven times — or multiples of seven — within any given *parasha.* See, for example, that the first verse in the Torah (Genesis 1:1) has seven words and twenty eight letters! (Other surprising examples can be found in my book *Studying the Torah* published by Jason Aronson Publishers.)

In our *parasha* (Verses 33-57) we find the word בית, with the definite article ה הידיעה (לבית, בבית, and הבית) a total of 28 times exactly. But if we include the word מבית (which does not have the definite article) we have a total of 29. Twenty-eight is the Torah's style, not twenty-nine. Granted that this is a mystical type of evidence, but it supports the contention that our word מבית is not similar to the other times בית is mentioned in this section. We conclude, therefore, as Rashi contends, that the word מבית does not mean "from the house" but rather "inside".

Rashi teaches us a subtle point, one often overlooked by translators.

Leviticus 16:2

וַיֹּאמֶר הי אֶל־מֹשֶׁה דַּבֵּר אֶל־אַהֲרֹן אָחִיךָ וְאַל־יָבֹא בְכָל־עֵת אֶל־
הַקֹּדֶשׁ מִבֵּית לַפָּרֹכֶת אֶל־פְּנֵי הַכַּפֹּרֶת אֲשֶׁר עַל־הָאָרֹן וְלֹא יָמוּת כִּי
בֶּעָנָן אֵרָאֶה עַל־הַכַּפֹּרֶת.

וְלֹא יָמוּת. שאם בא הוא מת.

And he will not die: *Rashi*: For if he comes (into the
Holy of Holies), he will die.

Certainly this is a strange comment!

YOUR QUESTION:

QUESTIONING RASHI

A Question: What has Rashi told us? This is obvious! Of course, if the Torah
says: "Do not go into the Holy of Holies and you will not die" then
clearly if you do go in, you will die. Too obvious to need mentioning.

Why then did Rashi mention it?

YOUR ANSWER:

WHAT IS BOTHERING RASHI?

An Answer: To understand Rashi we must remember his exquisite sensitivity
to the Hebrew language. He hears things that we take for granted.
Let us too try to "hear" the words closely.

"If you don't go in...you won't die." Is that so? The priest will
certainly die, maybe not now, but at sometime in the future he will

die; everyone dies, he is no exception. By not going into the Holy of Holies he has not guaranteed for himself an escape from death. But taken literally that is what the words of the Torah imply.

This is what Rashi comes to clarify.

How does his brief comment clarify matters?

Your Answer:

Understanding Rashi

An Answer: There is an overlooked subtlety here. The letter וֹ in the Tanach is usually translated as "and" and many English translations do so, yet this is frequently incorrect. The letter וֹ also has the meaning of "so that." That is its meaning here. "And he should not come at all times into the Holy place ...*so that* he not die."

This is precisely Rashi's lesson: "Don't go in *so that* you will not die, because if you go in you will die." But, of course, he may die for other reasons.

A Lesson

Rashi teaches us to pay close attention to each word, indeed, to each letter, in order to correctly understand what the Torah is saying.

Here we have an excellent example of the uniqueness of Rashi-comments. We see how every word of his comment is used with brilliant precision.

Leviticus 16:2,3. Same verse as above.

וַיֹּאמֶר הי אֶל־מֹשֶׁה דַּבֵּר אֶל־אַהֲרֹן אָחִיךָ וְאַל־יָבֹא בְכָל־עֵת אֶל־הַקֹּדֶשׁ מִבֵּית לַפָּרֹכֶת אֶל־פְּנֵי הַכַּפֹּרֶת אֲשֶׁר עַל־הָאָרֹן וְלֹא יָמוּת כִּי בֶּעָנָן אֵרָאֶה עַל־הַכַּפֹּרֶת. בְּזֹאת יָבֹא אַהֲרֹן אֶל־הַקֹּדֶשׁ בְּפַר בֶּן־בָּקָר לְחַטָּאת וְאַיִל לְעֹלָה.

כי בענן אראה. כי תמיד אני נראה שם עם עמוד עננ י ולפי שגלוי שכינתי שם יזהר שלא ירגיל לבא. זהו פשוטו. ומדרשו אל יבא כי אם בענן הקטרת ביום הכפורים.

For with a cloud I appear. *Rashi:* For I always appear there with My cloud-pillar. And because the revelation of My *Shechina* is there, he should take care that he not accustom himself to enter. That is the Simple Meaning (*p'shat*). But its *midrash* is: he may not enter (the Sanctuary) except with the cloud of incense on Yom Kippur.

WHAT HAS RASHI DONE

First let us look closely at this precisely crafted comment and see what Rashi has done. Then we will try understand why he has done it.

Notice how Rashi, in his *p'shat* interpretation, has rephrased each of the Torah's words with his own word or phrase.

The Torah's words	Rashi's words
כי	כי
בענן	עם עמוד ענני
אראה	תמיד אני נראה
———	———
כי	ולפי
אראה	שגילוי שכינתי שם
ואל יבא בכל עת...ולא ימות	יזהר שלא ירגיל לבא ...ולא ימות

Analyzing Rashi

The first part of this comment (which Rashi call *p'shat*) can be divided up into two parts. In the first half he rephrases the Torah's words; in the second half, he summarizes their significance.

The rephrasing:

1) The word אראה is in the future tense and should literally be translated "I will be seen." Rashi shows us that the correct meaning is not future, rather it is a verb that conveys continuous action; this Rashi does by rephrasing with the words תמיד אני נראה, "I always appear". We find other instances in the Torah where the future tense is used for continuous action.

2) The ב of the word בענן could mean either "*in* the cloud or "*with* the cloud" Rashi tells us that here it means "*with* the cloud."

3) The ב is vowelized with a *segol*, meaning "with *the* cloud" and not with a *shevah*, which would mean "with *a* cloud." *The* cloud refers to the cloud with which we are already familiar from the Exodus from Egypt. As it says: " *Hashem* went before by day in a **Pillar of Cloud** to lead them on the way," etc. (Exodus 13:21). This was *Hashem*'s own pillar of cloud. Thus Rashi rephrases it: עם עמוד ענני "the pillar of *My* cloud."

After Rashi has clarified the meaning of the individual words, he then reviews the idea to tell us their significance. This cloud is an indication of G-d's presence, His *Shechina*; it then follows that one must be extra cautious about entering the Holy of Holies. The High Priest may enter there only when explicitly permitted.

4) The previous words in this verse ואל יבא בכל עת are not clear. Do they mean:

1) He should not come *any time* (which means: never) or

2) He should not come *at any time* (which means: he may not enter whenever he feels like it.)

Rashi tells us that "he is warned *not to accustom himself to enter regularly*." That is #2 above. He may come into the Holy of Holies (he does enter on Yom Kippur) but since *Hashem's Shechina* is there, he should be careful not to treat this casually and not to "accustom himself to enter regularly".

In summary: Rashi is telling us that the verse means that the High Priest should not enter the Holy of Holies at just any time because G-d's *Shechina* is there. He may only enter on Yom Kippur.

Questioning Rashi

But isn't this what the verse itself says? What has Rashi added? Why has he gone to all this trouble just to tell us what we already know? What is bothering him?

Your Answer:

What Is Bothering Rashi?

An Answer: Rashi frequently comments on verses that have the word כי in them. See, for example, his comment to Genesis 50:19. He is fascinated by this little word. In the Talmud (tractate *Gitin* 90a) the Sage, Reish Lakish, has explained that this word has four different meanings. Rashi's comment there is one of his longest comments in the Talmud. This shows his interest in this particular matter and is characteristic of Rashi's interest in understanding the nuances of the Hebrew language. Since this word has several meanings, Rashi is concerned that we clearly understand its correct meaning wherever its meaning is unclear in the Torah.

The Question is: What does כי mean here? If it means "because," which it would seem to mean, then what do these words mean: "He should not enter at any time ...*because* in a cloud I will appear"? We ask: So what if G-d appears in a cloud? Is that a reason for not entering the Holy of Holies? Or, to put the question another way: If G-d appeared *without* a cloud, would the High Priest then be allowed to enter? Certainly not! This is what is bothering Rashi, the word "because" seems to give the wrong "cause". For this reason Rashi rephrases the verse to overcome this possible misunderstanding.

How does Rashi's first explanation — *p'shat* — clarify matters?

Your Answer:

Understanding Rashi

An Answer: Rashi is telling us that the cloud is an incidental fact. In effect he is saying to put the matter of the cloud aside, the real issue is that G-d's *Shechina* is there. This is the reason that in Rashi's summary he leaves out all mention of the cloud, referring only to the *Shechina*, because that is the essential factor. Now the word כי "because" makes sense; "do not enter...because My *Shechina* is there..."

A Closer Look

Now notice another subtle change that Rashi has made in his rephrasing which you may have missed before. Rashi has כי תמיד אני נראה שם עם עמוד ענני.

Look at the order of words here. First comes "I always appear (the *Shechina*)" then comes "with the pillar of My cloud." In the Torah, on the hand, mention of the cloud comes first, right after "because." This is certainly significant. It is Rashi's subtle way of reinforcing the idea that the causal factor for not entering the Holy of Holies is the presence of G-d's *Shechina* (which in Rashi's rephrasing comes right after "because") and NOT the presence of the cloud (which in the Torah's phrasing does come right after "because.")

A Lesson

This alone should teach us: We should never, never, take Rashi's words or the sequence in which he orders them, for granted!

But we have not yet finished analyzing this exquisite comment. What of the second interpretation, which Rashi calls *midrash*? Let us look at it and see what it reveals.

What Does the *Drash* Say?

The *drash* interprets the verse completely different. The cloud here is the cloud of incense burning on the coals. See verse 13 where the Torah says explicitly that the High Priest, on Yom Kippur, places the incense on the fire and creates a cloud of the burning incense which fills the Holy of Holies. That is what Rashi also says here. "He may not (ever) enter (the Sanctuary) כי *except* in the cloud of incense on Yom Kippur."

Now let us compare the meaning of the words in our verse according to the *drash* and we will see how they differ from Rashi's first — *p'shat* — rephrasing. We will also see the deeper significance of Rashi's precise rephrasing in the *p'shat* interpretation.

P'shat	*Drash*
ואל תבוא בכל עת =	
he should not come *at any time*	he should not come *any time*
כי =	
because	except

בענן =

    with My cloud-pillar   in the cloud of incense

אראה =

    am I continuously seen there   I will be (permitted to be) seen
                                           (on Yom Kippur)

Now we see why Rashi rephrased the words in his first — *p'shat* — interpretation, he did so in order to emphasize how different they are from the *drash* interpretation. In fact, *each* word in the *p'shat* interpretation has a different meaning from its *drash* meaning.

P'SHAT AND DRASH

Now we must understand why Rashi considers the second interpretation *drash* and the first one *p'shat*. At first glance this is strange. Certainly what he calls the *drash* interpretation is factually true. In verse 13 below, we see that the High Priest *does* create a cloud of smoke from the burning incense. So why is this *drash*? The High Priest is inside the Holy of Holies with a cloud of burning incense; the cloud is one of incense and is not G-d's *Shechina*. This would seem to be more *p'shat* than what Rashi calls *p'shat*!

What evidence would you cite to support Rashi's claim that the *p'shat* meaning of ענן in our verse is G-d's pillar-cloud and not the incense cloud?

Hint: Look closely at the whole context.

YOUR ANSWER:

UNDERSTANDING RASHI'S P'SHAT

An Answer: Several reasons have been given for Rashi considering the cloud to be the *Shechina* as the Simple Meaning and not the cloud of incense.

    * If it were the latter, the Torah should have been explicit and said "the cloud of incense" as it does in verse 13.

    * Mention of the incense ceremony should come *after* the phrase בזאת יבא אהרן "with this shall Aaron come..." and not before it. Because the words "With this shall Aaron come..." emphasize the manner in which the High Priest may enter the Holy of Holies. The cloud of incense was one of the conditions which allowed him to enter, it should have been listed with the other conditions mentioned " a bull ...".

* And in fact it is mentioned later in verse 13 among those requirements for entering the Holy of Holies. Why then is it mentioned here at all ?

For all these reasons, Rashi understands the *p'shat* meaning of the ענן to be the *Shechina* rather than the cloud of smoke from the burning incense.

A STRANGE *DRASH*

When we seek out Rashi's *drash* we find something strange indeed. It is to be found in the Talmud, tractate *Yoma* 53a. There it says the following:

" 'And he shall place the incense on the fire before *Hashem...*' (verse 16:13). He may not prepare (the incense) outside and then enter. This (say our Sages) is to teach us not to follow the Sadducees' interpretation, who say: He should prepare the incense outside and then enter. (The Sadducees asked) Which verse teaches this? 'Because with a cloud I may be seen on the *Kaporus*' (note: this is our verse) this teaches us (say the Sadducees) that he should prepare the incense outside and then enter."

Our Rabbis rejected the Sadducee interpretation of the words כי בענן" "אראה על הכפורת.

This means that the *drash* that Rashi cites, that the cloud is of incense, has its basis in a *drash* of the Sadducees! This is amazing.

THE SADDUCEES

The Sadducees were the antagonists of our Sages, the P'rushim, during the Talmudic period. They did not accept the Oral Tradition (what is called *drash*) and they interpreted the Torah without reliance on it. They dealt only with what seemed to them to be *p'shat*. Why would Rashi quote them, of all people? And why would Rashi refer to this as *drash* when it is based on a Sadducian idea, they who vehemently opposed any form of *drash*!? Doubly strange indeed.

RASHI HOISTS THEM ON THEIR OWN PETARD!

That's precisely Rashi's point! Rashi certainly knew this was based on a Sadducian idea. Rashi is fully aware of the Sadducee thought on this verse, his Talmud commentary includes tractate *Yoma* where this *drash* is quoted, but Rashi isn't accepting it, he is intentionally undermining it. The Sadducees claim to deal only in *p'shat*, yet Rashi points out that their view is certainly not *p'shat* (for the reasons I have outlined above). Rashi perhaps mockingly refers to their view as *drash*, which is anathema to the Sadducees. He does this precisely in order to delegitimize their interpretation.

But we must remember, Rashi refers to their view as *drash* only in the sense that it is not *p'shat*; but it is not *drash* in the sense that it was an interpretation of our Talmudic Rabbis, because it certainly was not.

Leviticus 18:28

וְלֹא־תָקִיא הָאָרֶץ אֶתְכֶם בְּטַמַּאֲכֶם אֹתָהּ כַּאֲשֶׁר קָאָה אֶת־הַגּוֹי אֲשֶׁר לִפְנֵיכֶם.

ולא תקיא הארץ אתכם. משל לבן מלך שהאכילוהו דבר מאוס שאין עומד במעיו אלא מקיאו. כך ארץ ישראל אינה מקיימת עוברי עבירה.

And the land shall not vomit you out: *Rashi*: This can be compared to a prince whom they fed something repulsive, which his stomach could not retain and he vomitted it out. So too Eretz Yisrael cannot retain sinners.

Rashi gives us a parable which is taken from the *midrash*, to explain his point.

What would you ask?

YOUR QUESTION:

QUESTIONING RASHI

A Question: The parable compares the sensitivity that the Land of Israel has to sinners that dwell in its midst to the sensitivity that a refined prince has to disgusting food. Both violently expel the ingested matter.

But what does the parable teach us that we wouldn't know from the verse itself?

Note: It must be said that Rashi often quotes parables in his commentary and it is not always easy to understand what they add to our understanding. Many times he will just tell us the beginning of the parable without finishing it. See, for example, the Rashi's on the following verses: Leviticus 11:2; Numbers 11:5; Genesis 49:20. When he does this we can speculate that his aim is to have us look up the source ourselves, to put out the energy in order to appreciate the parable. But in our case he tells us the whole parable from beginning to end. Why? Why is it so important?

Is something bothering him? What?

You must read the verse in Hebrew to find the subtlety.

YOUR ANSWER:

WHAT IS BOTHERING RASHI?

An Answer: There is a problem with understanding our verse; a problem that is rarely noticed. Let us see our verse in context:

יח:כו. וּשְׁמַרְתֶּם אַתֶּם אֶת־חֻקֹּתַי וְאֶת־מִשְׁפָּטַי וְלֹא תַעֲשׂוּ מִכֹּל הַתּוֹעֵבֹת הָאֵלֶּה הָאֶזְרָח וְהַגֵּר הַגָּר בְּתוֹכֲכֶם.

כז. כִּי אֶת־כָּל־הַתּוֹעֵבֹת הָאֵל עָשׂוּ אַנְשֵׁי־הָאָרֶץ אֲשֶׁר לִפְנֵיכֶם וַתִּטְמָא הָאָרֶץ.

כח. וְלֹא־תָקִיא הָאָרֶץ אֶתְכֶם בְּטַמַּאֲכֶם אֹתָהּ כַּאֲשֶׁר קָאָה אֶת־הַגּוֹי אֲשֶׁר לִפְנֵיכֶם.

18:26 "You shall keep My decrees and My judgments and not commit any of these abominations, the native or the proselyte who lives among you.

18:27 For all these abominations were done by the inhabitants of the Land who were before you and the Land became contaminated.

18:28 **And the Land will not vomit you out when you contaminate it as it had vomited out the nation that was before you."**

Read this way, we come to a strange conclusion: The Land will *not* vomit you out if you contaminate it, as it had vomited out the nation before you. This is very strange indeed.

Rashi's parable comes to reject this reading.

How does it?

אחרי מות

YOUR ANSWER

Understanding Rashi

An Answer: The parable tells us that the Land, due to its spiritual sensitivity, will throw out the sinners, Israelites included, because, like a sensitive stomach, it cannot "stomach" immoral behavior.

But we must ask: Why is this the correct reading of the verse. The verse seems to say the opposite when it says: ...ולא תקיא הארץ אתכם "And the Land will *not* vomit you out..."

A More Thorough Understanding

An Answer: Our answer is similar to what we said above in verse 16:2. That is, that the letter ו can have several meanings, "and" being just one of them.

It can also mean "or", as in Exodus 21:15:

וּמַכֵּה אָבִיו וְאִמּוֹ מוֹת יוּמָת.
"One who strikes his father *or* his mother shall surely be put to death.

It can also mean "so that" and that is what it means in our verse: "Don't do these abominations *so that* the Land will not vomit you out..."

A Deeper Analysis

But, if we are to appreciate Rashi fully, we must ask another critical question:

How does Rashi know that this ו means "so that" and not " and"?

Can you find support for this here or anywhere in the Torah?

YOUR ANSWER:

A Deeper Understanding

An Answer: The meaning cannot be "and you will not be vomited out of the Land..." for the following reasons:

125 —

1. If we look at verse 20:22 the meaning is clearer: There it says:

וּשְׁמַרְתֶּם אֶת־כָּל־חֻקֹּתִי וְאֶת־כָּל־מִשְׁפָּטַי וַעֲשִׂיתֶם אֹתָם וְלֹא־תָקִיא
אֶתְכֶם הָאָרֶץ אֲשֶׁר אֲנִי מֵבִיא אֶתְכֶם שָׁמָּה לָשֶׁבֶת בָּהּ.

"You shall observe all My decrees and all My ordinances
and perform them *so that* the Land to which I bring you
to dwell will not vomit you out."

The implication is clear: Otherwise you will be vomited out.

2. We know as a matter of fact that the people were exiled —"vomited out" — of the Land. If G-d's promise was that they would not
be exiled, it wasn't fulfilled!

3. We also find other verses that speak of expulsion from the Land.
See for example Leviticus 26:41.

For all of these reasons Rashi probably came to his decision that the
correct meaning of our verse was as indicated by the parable which he
cites from the *midrash.*

Now let us look at something very interesting which shows Rashi's original use of *midrash.*

RASHI AND THE *MIDRASH* _____

The source of the parable that Rashi cites is found in *Toras Cohanim,* a
midrashic source frequently used by Rashi in his commentary to
Leviticus. But what is unusual is that the *midrash* gives this comment
not on this verse, but on a verse at the end of *parashas Kedoshim!* The
parable is brought as a comment to verse 20:22, which we just quoted
above.

Why does Rashi use it here and not there, as the *midrash* itself does?
Why does Rashi make this switch?

Can you think of a reason?

Hint: Compare the two verse, 18:28 with 20:22.

YOUR ANSWER:

UNDERSTANDING RASHI'S USE OF *MIDRASH* _____

Let us compare the two verses and look for subtle differences:

The verse in *Kedoshim* says:

וּשְׁמַרְתֶּם אֶת־כָּל־חֻקֹּתַי וְאֶת־כָּל־מִשְׁפָּטַי וַעֲשִׂיתֶם אֹתָם וְלֹא־תָקִיא **אֶתְכֶם הָאָרֶץ** אֲשֶׁר אֲנִי מֵבִיא אֶתְכֶם שָׁמָּה לָשֶׁבֶת בָּהּ.

Our verse says:

וְלֹא־תָקִיא הָאָרֶץ אֶתְכֶם בְּטַמַּאֲכֶם אֹתָהּ כַּאֲשֶׁר קָאָה אֶת־הַגּוֹי אֲשֶׁר לִפְנֵיכֶם.

What is the difference?

Answer: Our verse says: "The Land will not vomit you out" the other verse says: "You will not be vomited out by the Land."

There is a rule in Torah interpretation which teaches us that we must be sensitive to the order of words in each verse. By placing a word earlier in a verse, the Torah wants to emphasize that word. Did you notice that in our verse the word הארץ comes before the word אתכם; while in *Kedoshim* the word אתכם comes before הארץ. This indicates that in our verse the issue of the Land is foremost, while in *Kedoshim* the issue of the people being removed from the Land is foremost. A subtle difference, but a difference nevertheless. It is likely that Rashi moved the *midrash* from its original place in *Kedoshim* to our verse for this very reason. Here the sensitivity of the Land is the issue and that is the whole point of the parable.

A Lesson

In his Torah commentary, Rashi may change the location of a *midrash*. There is always a reason for his doing this. It our job to try to understand the reason.

פרשת קדושים

Sensitivity to Rashi's choice of words is necessary to fully understand his message.

Leviticus 19:2

דַּבֵּר אֶל־כָּל־עֲדַת בְּנֵי־יִשְׂרָאֵל וְאָמַרְתָּ אֲלֵהֶם קְדֹשִׁים תִּהְיוּ כִּי קָדוֹשׁ אֲנִי ה׳ אֱלֹקֵיכֶם.

קְדֹשִׁים תִּהְיוּ. הֱווּ פְרוּשִׁים מִן הָעֲרָיוֹת וּמִן הָעֲבֵירָה שֶׁכָּל מָקוֹם שֶׁאַתָּה מוֹצֵא גֶדֶר עֶרְוָה אַתָּה מוֹצֵא קְדוּשָׁה. אִשָּׁה זוֹנָה וַחֲלָלָה וְגוֹ׳ (ויקרא כא:ז) אֲנִי ה׳ מְקַדִּשְׁכֶם (שם ח׳) וְלֹא יְחַלֵּל זַרְעוֹ כִּי אֲנִי ה׳ מְקַדְּשׁוֹ (שם טו).

You shall be holy: *Rashi:* Keep aloof from the forbidden sexual relations (mentioned above) and from sinful thoughts. Because wherever you find [in the Torah] a command to fence yourself off from sexual immorality you also find mention of 'holiness.' (Some examples:) "They shall not take a wife that is a harlot, or a profane woman, etc." (Lev. 21:7) and the next verse "I am *Hashem*, Who sanctifies you." And "Neither shall he profane his seed....for I am *Hashem* Who sanctifies him." (ibid. 15).

WHAT IS RASHI SAYING?

Rashi tells us that "holiness" here means observing the sexual code of forbidden relationships. This he undoubtedly derives from the fact that our verse comes on the heels of the last *parasha*, where the laws of the forbidden incestuous relations are commanded.

He supports this idea by citing several verses where the laws of sexual relations are given and which are immediately followed by G-d's statement of holiness. We should note that all the cases cited by Rashi are sexual relations that are forbidden only to priests.

With this in mind what can you ask of Rashi?

YOUR QUESTION:

QUESTIONING RASHI

A Question: First of all, why does Rashi bring as evidence only cases of priestly restrictions. Certainly the ordinary Israelite also has sexual prohibitions, why aren't these cited? Secondly, there are quite a few places where the Torah forbids sexual relations and yet there is no mention of holiness. The previous *parasha*, *Achrai Mos* (Chapter 18), lists over a dozen forbidden sexual relations and yet no mention is made of "holiness." Also in Deuteronomy, where the *mamzer* is forbidden, (Deut. 23: 3) there is no mention of holiness.

This is certainly strange and seems to seriously undermine Rashi's point.

How can we understand this?

To understand this you must look carefully at Rashi's words.

YOUR ANSWER:

UNDERSTANDING RASHI

An Answer: At the outset, I should say that I couldn't find any commentary who relates to this question. The question and answer were given to me by a Jerusalemite by the name of Rav Aaron Moshe Schwartz.

Rashi says "Any place that you find the גדר ("restrictions") of sexual relations...you find holiness." Note that Rashi doesn't say "sexual relations" rather גדר ערוה. A גדר is a fence; so this means restrictions beyond the ordinary restrictions, which are intended to fence one off one from even approaching a forbidden act. It is only the priest who has these added restrictions; it is only from the laws of sexual purity of the priest that Rashi can bring evidence to the point he wants to make. The Talmud (*Kedushin* 31a) says that the Torah placed a stricter code of conduct on the priests.

It is for this reason that Rashi only uses examples from the priests, because they are particularly commanded to restrict themselves from certain sexual relations, above and beyond those which are required of every Jew. This is the sign of their holiness.

That is what Rashi means when he says at the beginning of his comment הוו פרושים מן העריות, "separate yourselves from sexual sins." Holiness comes not from merely observing the laws regarding the forbidden sexual relations, but rather from keeping clear of any hint of sexual impropriety. That is holiness. This coincides with the basic meaning of the word קדושה which translates : "to be separate." *Hashem* is קדוש because He is separate from anything we can imagine. The Jew becomes קדוש when he builds a fence around forbidden acts in order to guarantee his separation from them.

We see how Rashi is precise in his choice of words in order to make this important and fundamental point.

P'shat and drash combine to give us the fuller meaning of the verse.

Leviticus 19: 3

אִישׁ אִמּוֹ וְאָבִיו תִּירָאוּ וְאֶת שַׁבְּתֹתַי תִּשְׁמֹרוּ אֲנִי הי אֱלֹקֵיכֶם.

אִישׁ אִמּוֹ וְאָבִיו תִּירָאוּ. כָּל אֶחָד מִכֶּם תִּירְאוּ אָבִיו וְאִמּוֹ, זֶהוּ פְּשׁוּטוֹ. וּמִדְרָשׁוֹ אֵין לִי אֶלָּא אִישׁ, אִשָּׁה מִנַּיִן? כְּשֶׁהוּא אוֹמֵר תִּירָאוּ הֲרֵי כָּאן שְׁנַיִם אִם כֵּן לָמָּה נֶאֱמַר אִישׁ? שֶׁהָאִישׁ סִפֵּק בְּיָדוֹ לַעֲשׂוֹת, אֲבָל אִשָּׁה רְשׁוּת אֲחֵרִים עָלֶיהָ.

Every man shall fear his mother and his father: *Rashi*: Each one of you shall fear his father and his mother. This is its Simple Meaning. Its *midrash* [however, says]: I only know [the law] that a male אִישׁ [is obligated to fear his parents]. Whence do I know that a woman is also [obligated]? Because it says "you (plural) shall fear" it is evident therefore that it refers to two people (man and woman). Why then does it say אִישׁ "man"? Because it is only the man who has the means to do it, while the woman is under the control of others (a married woman must have her husband's consent).

As you can see, Rashi offers both *p'shat* and halachic *drash* on this verse.

What would you ask here?

YOUR QUESTION:

QUESTIONING RASHI

A Question: Why? Why is his *p'shat* interpretation needed; he seems to be saying the same thing the Torah verse itself says. What does it add to my understanding? And why the need for two interpretations, *p'shat* and *drash*?

What's bothering Rashi here?

YOUR ANSWER:

WHAT IS BOTHERING RASHI?

An Answer: This verse is an odd grammatical mix. It begins with the *singular*, איש אמו "*a* man *his* mother..." and ends with the *plural* תיראו, "*you* (plural) shall fear." Rashi's comment is meant to deal with this. How?

YOUR ANSWER:

UNDERSTANDING RASHI

An Answer: Remember, Moses is speaking to the whole assembly of Israel. He addresses all of them as a group, as he tells them the law for the individual. He says to them "each and every *one* (singular) *of you* (plural) assembled here should fear *his* mother and *his* father."

In this way Rashi has explained the odd singular/plural combination.

A CLOSER LOOK

Rashi adds the word מכם. Why? What does this add to our understanding?

YOUR ANSWER:

An Answer: With this one word Rashi deals with a second grammatical problem as well. Besides the singular/plural discrepancy, there is also a third person (his)/second person (you) discrepancy. The verse speaks in the third person "each man *his* mother..." Then it switches to second person "*You* shall fear." By inserting the word מכם which is second person, plural, Rashi bridges the gap between the third person pronoun and the second person. Moses is speaking to the people and says "Each man כל אחד (singular) of *you* מכם (plural) shall fear *his* (third person) mother etc." In this way the apparent discrepancy dissolves.

Rashi's second interpretation is from a *midrash halacha*.

UNDERSTANDING THE *MIDRASH*

The *midrash* deals with the singular/plural tension in a different way. The plural verb תיראו teaches us that both men and women are obligated to fear their parents. But if both are equally included in this mitzvah, why, one may ask, is the singular used at all? The singular, the *midrash* says, teaches us that while a woman is obligated to fulfill the mitzvah of respecting her parents, this has limits. If she is married, her first obligation is to her husband and that may restrict her ability to honor her parents. Men, on the other hand, are always under the obligation to fulfill this mitzvah; this is the reason the verse uses the singular term איש.

WHY TWO INTERPRETATIONS?

Remember, that the commentaries on Rashi always make a point of understanding why Rashi needed to cite a second interpretation, that of *drash*, once he has already explained the verse according to the *p'shat*. What weakness is there in the *p'shat* interpretation that requires another interpretation?

YOUR ANSWER:

A DEEPER UNDERSTANDING

An Answer: If the Torah only wanted to tell us that every individual is obligated to fear his parents, then the *mitzvah* could have been phrased without using the word איש at all. It could have simply said, for example, את אביכם ואת אמכם תיראו. Therefore the *drash* explains that the word איש is necessary because it teaches us that the man has more of an obligation than does the woman.

(See *Misiach Ilmim*)

A REMAINING QUESTION

Rashi's phrasing is a bit strange. He writes כל אחד מכם **תיראו אביו ואמו**, "each one of you shall *fear his father and mother*." This is not the order that we find in our verse! Rashi reverses the location of the word תיראו,

placing it before "his father and mother" and not after, as in the verse.

Can you see why?

YOUR ANSWER:

An Answer: Since Rashi inserted the word מכם to be a bridge to the second person plural, he placed it immediately next to the word תראו which is a second person plural verb.

(See *Mizrachi*)

A REMAINING PUZZLE

But Rashi also reverses the order of the parents! In the Torah it says "his mother and his father" but Rashi has "his father and his mother." Why?

Why would Rashi switch the order? I don't know.

Can you think of a reasonable explanation?

If you can, I'd be very interested in hearing your explanation.

Rashi makes a subtle grammatical point which has an important ethical lesson.

Leviticus 19:13

לֹא־תַעֲשֹׁק אֶת־רֵעֲךָ וְלֹא תִגְזֹל לֹא־תָלִין פְּעֻלַּת שָׂכִיר אִתְּךָ עַד־בֹּקֶר.

לֹא תָלִין: לשון נקבה מוסב על הפעולה.

It shall not abide: *Rashi:* [The word תלין] is feminine gender and refers to [the feminine noun] "wages."

WHAT IS RASHI SAYING?

Rashi makes an important grammatical point. The meaning of the word תלין is ambiguous. The prefix letter ת can mean one of two things:

1) *You* shall not cause to abide (2nd person singular).

2) *It* (the wages) shall not abide (3rd person singular feminine).

Rashi tells us that the correct translation here is choice #2. According to Rashi the verse is to be translated: "You shall not oppress your fellow man nor rob him; *the wages of a hired man shall not abide* by you until morning."

But then, considering the whole verse, you should have a question on Rashi.

Hint: Look at the whole verse.

YOUR QUESTION:

QUESTIONING RASHI _____

A Question: The verse used the prefix ת previously in this verse to mean "you" (*You* shall not oppress, *you* shall not rob). Why does Rashi switch, in mid-verse, the meaning of the ת prefix from "you" to "it" (wages)?

You must be somewhat familiar with Hebrew grammar to answer this one. Can you?

There are several reasons that forced Rashi to make the choice he did.

What are they?

YOUR ANSWER:

UNDERSTANDING RASHI _____

Some Answers:

1)   If the meaning were "You shall not let the wages abide..." Then the Hebrew should have added the word את before the direct object "wages." In biblical Hebrew the את is placed before the direct object.
        Like this:

        לא תלין **את** פעולת שכיר וגו׳

2)   The words "You shall not let abide..." imply intentionality, that is: You shall not keep the hired man's wages until morning (on purpose). But if that were the correct meaning, then the word אתך "with you" is redundant. Where else would you keep it, if not "with you"?! It would have been more appropriate and less wordy to say:

        לא תלין את פעולת שכיר עד הבקר.

135 —

The addition of the word "with you" implies that it remained "with you" by accident or due to forgetfulness.

3) It has been pointed out that the Hebrew verb לין ("to stay over-night") in the Tanach is always in the intransitive form, meaning "to stay overnight" and never in the transitive, which would mean "to cause to stay overnight." So here too it should be translated "to stay overnight."

4) We must say that the prohibition is not against intentional with-holding wages. If it were speaking of intentionally withholding one's wages it would be identical with the prohibition of לא תעשק in this verse which Rashi tells us means "do not withhold the wages of a hired man." Therefore if it is referring to unintentional and inconsiderate forgetting to pay a workers' wages on time, the phras-ing "It shall not abide with you..." is appropriate.

For these reasons Rashi chose to interpret the words לא תלין as meaning "the wages shall not remain with you overnight."

A Deeper Look

But if the prohibition is against unintentional forgetting, you should have a question.

What would you ask?

Your Question:

A Question: How can the Torah prohibit an *unintentional* act? By definition, the person did not do the transgression on purpose, so how can it be prohibited and if transgressed, why should the person be pun-ished?

You Answer:

An Answer: This is precisely the point. The Torah makes us aware of the even-tuality of forgetting to pay a workman on time. By making a per-son culpable for such inconsiderate forgetting, the Torah increases the chance that the person will be careful to be more considerate and less forgetful.

(See *Be'er Rechovos*)

❖❖❖

Rashi chooses from his midrashic source that which best suits his exegetical goals.

Leviticus 19:14

לֹא־תְקַלֵּל חֵרֵשׁ וְלִפְנֵי עִוֵּר לֹא תִתֵּן מִכְשֹׁל וְיָרֵאתָ מֵּאֱלֹקֶיךָ אֲנִי הי.

וְלִפְנֵי עִוֵּר לֹא תִתֵּן מִכְשֹׁל. לִפְנֵי הסומא בדבר לא תתן עצה שאינה הוגנת לו, אל תאמר מכור שדך וקח לך חמור ואתה עוקף עליו ונוטלה הימנו.

וְיָרֵאתָ מֵאֱלֹקֶיךָ. לפי שהדבר הזה אינו מסור לבריות לידע אם דעתו של זה לטובה או לרעה ויכול להשמט ולומר לטובה נתכוונתי לפיכך נאמר בו ויראת מאלקיך המכיר מחשבותיך. וכן כל דבר המסור ללבו של אדם העושהו ואין שאר הבריות מכירות בו, נאמר ויראת מאלקיך.

And before a blind person you shall not place a stumbling block: *Rashi*: Before someone who is "blind" in the matter you shall not give advice which is not fair to him. Don't say to him "sell your field and buy a donkey" while you are outsmarting him to take it from him.

And you shall fear your G-d. *Rashi*: Because it is not given to human beings to know whether his intention was for good or evil and he could therefore evade [responsibility] and say "I intended it for his benefit" therefore it says concerning it "you shall fear your G-d," Who knows your thoughts. Likewise every matter which is given over to the heart of the person who does the action and no one else could possibly know [his true intentions] it says "fear your G-d."

Clearly Rashi has taken the meaning of this verse out of its simple meaning and given it a more allegorical meaning.

YOUR QUESTION:

QUESTIONING RASHI

A Question: Why does Rashi ignore the literal meaning and chose this interpretation?

Can you think of a reason?

Hint: Look closely at the wording in the verse and also at Rashi's second comment.

WHAT IS BOTHERING RASHI?

An Answer: Some commentators (*Mishmeres Hakodesh*) point out the unusual use of the word תתן which literally means "to give." It is strange in this context. A more appropriate word would have been לא תשים "do not place." The word "give" is akin to "giving advice" And this is exactly what Rashi says לא תתן עצה. The fact that he uses the word תתן in his commentary (repeating the Torah's word) gives one the feeling that he is stressing the centrality of this word.

Another explanation has been given by the *Gur Aryeh*. Note that in Rashi's second comment he says this is a sin that cannot be detected by others, only by G-d. If one places a stone on the street in the way of a blind person, this could certainly be seen by others and understood as a malicious deed. Therefore Rashi sought an example in which the behavior alone could be interpreted as innocent. Like giving bad advice (good people do it all the time!).

RASHI AND THE *MIDRASH*

The source of Rashi's comment is the *midrash Toras Cohanim*. There it says the following:

"Before someone who is 'blind' in the matter. If someone asks you if a certain woman is permissible for a priest to marry, don't say she is, when you know she is not. If a man asks your advice, don't give advice which is not fair to him. Don't say to him: Go out early in the morning when you know he may be attacked by robbers. Don't say: Go out at noon when he may get sunstroke. Don't say: Sell your field and buy a donkey instead, when you really intend to outsmart him and take [his field] from him."

We see that the *midrash* offers several examples of "putting a stumbling block before a blind man." Rashi chooses only one. Can you sense why he chose only this one?

But first we must try to understand the *midrash*.

UNDERSTANDING THE *MIDRASH*

Taken literally our verse speaks of a case where a person intentionally caused the hapless blind person to stumble and fall, the villian having no ulterior motive besides the sadistic pleasure of watching him suffer. It is really unusual for the Torah to point out such malicious behaviors and see the need to explicitly prohibit them.

If, on the hand, we think through this commandment we can understand its deeper intent. Although the Torah does not say so explicitly, it certainly would prohibit putting a stumbling block before a sighted person, or cursing a person who can hear. These too are forbidden. Why then were the deaf and the blind singled out here? The point obviously is to emphasize the evil in taking advantage of the disadvantaged person. Once we keep this in mind, we understand that the *midrashim* are in fact offering us a *p'shat* application of the verse. For all the cases in the *midrash* exemplify the deeper meaning of the mitzvah, that is taking advantage of an innocent, unprotected individual.

But we are still left with the question:

Why did Rashi choose the one case he did from those quoted by the *midrash*?

YOUR ANSWER:

UNDERSTANDING RASHI'S CHOICE OF *MIDRASH*

An Answer: All the cases cited by the *midrash* are instances of a person spitefully causing harm to another person. Only in the *midrash*'s case of buying the man's field after he was seduced to sell it, does the culprit benefit from "the stumbling block" that he set. Our verse exists in a context of verses of transgressions which describe harm brought to another where the sinner benefits. ("Don't withold wages of your fellow man, don't rob" etc.) It is reasonable that Rashi sought a similar case where the stumbling block not only caused harm to the victim but also took advantage of him to the benefit of the sinner.

THE LESSON

Rashi chose that part of the *midrash* that served his needs as commentator to explain the deeper meaning of the Torah's words in the context in which they are found. Of course every case in a *midrash-halacha* is important to know as a lesson in correct behavior, but when they less easily blend into the Torah's words, Rashi is not likely to make use of them.

A typical two-interpretation comment. Understanding the reason for both, is the challenge.

Leviticus 19:15

לֹא־תַעֲשׂוּ עָוֶל בַּמִּשְׁפָּט לֹא־תִשָּׂא פְנֵי־דָל וְלֹא תֶהְדַּר פְּנֵי גָדוֹל בְּצֶדֶק תִּשְׁפֹּט עֲמִיתֶךָ.

בצדק תשפט עמיתך. כמשמעו. דבר אחר, הוי דן את חברך לכף זכות.

With righteousness you shall judge your fellow. *Rashi:* Take this as its plain meaning. Another interpretation: Judge your fellow favorably.

Rashi's *Midrashic* Source

Rashi's source is found in the Talmud tractate *Shavuouth* 30a:

> " 'With righteousness you shall judge your fellow.' One (litigant) should not be allowed to sit while the other stands, one speaks as much as he wants, while the other is told 'Be brief.' Another interpretation: judge your fellow favorably."

We see that Rashi has abbreviated the Talmudic quote. The specific examples of the first interpretation (sitting versus standing, freedom to talk versus restricted speech) are summed up in one word — "כמשמעו", "Take it as its plain meaning." Which Rashi feels is the plain sense of the words "with righteousness you shall judge your fellow." The verse tells us how justice is to be administered — how the courtroom proceedings should be conducted as a man is being judged. The reference is not the judgment itself, which certainly must be done according to the rules of righteousness. We see what Rashi means by his term כמשמעו. It means, be equally fair to each litigant when you sit in judgment over him. Rashi felt the specifics were not necessary — the meaning is clear.

The second interpretation is a direct quote from the Talmudic source.

Considering the two interpretations that Rashi cites, what would you ask?

Your Question:

Questioning Rashi

A Question: Why does Rashi need an additional interpretation, when the first one seems to be the simple *p'shat*?

Is something problematic with the first one?

What's bothering Rashi with his first interpretation?

YOUR ANSWER:

WHAT IS BOTHERING RASHI?

An Answer: The first interpretation considers this a command to judges. But the verse says "your fellow" which implies an equal relationship among the individuals.

How does the second interpretation overcome this difficulty?

YOUR ANSWER:

UNDERSTANDING RASHI

An Answer: This interpretation speaks of everyday situations where we judge our friends, not in a court of law, of course, but in the courtroom of our mind. Here the Torah tells us to be fair in our mental judgment; give your fellowman the benefit of the doubt.

But, then we can ask: If the second interpretation is superior to the first, why offer the first one at all?

Can you see a weakness in the second interpretation?

YOUR ANSWER:

A FULLER UNDERSTANDING

An Answer: The whole context of this verse is geared to the judge who sits in court and passes judgment ("You shall not commit injustice in judgment, you shall not favor a poor man and you shall not show honor to a powerful man."). Thus the strength of the first interpretation is that it also refers to a judge's behavior in line with the context of the verse.

(See *Maskil L'Dovid*)

In what appears to be a simple parable, we see the precision of the Sages' thinking.

Leviticus 19: 18

לֹא־תִקֹּם וְלֹא־תִטֹּר אֶת־בְּנֵי עַמֶּךָ וְאָהַבְתָּ לְרֵעֲךָ כָּמוֹךָ אֲנִי ה'.

לֹא תִקֹּם. אמר לו השאילני מגלך אמר לו לאו! למחר אמר לו השאילני קרדומך. אמר לו איני משאילך כדרך שלא השאלתני, זו היא נקימה. ואיזו היא נטירה? אמר לו השאילני את קרדומך אמר לו לאו. למחר אמר לו השאילני מגלך אמר לו הא לך! איני כמותך שלא השאלתני. זו היא נטירה. שנוטר האיבה בלבו אף על פי שאינו נוקם.

You shall not take revenge: *Rashi:* He (A) said to him [B]: "Lend me your scythe." The other (B) says: "No." The next day B says: "Lend me your ax." A says "I will not lend it to you just as you did not lend me [your scythe]." This is taking revenge. What is bearing a grudge? A said "Lend me your ax." B says "No." The next day B says to A, "Lend me your scythe." A says, "Here it is. See, I am not like you, who did not lend me [your ax]!" This is bearing a grudge, he keeps the hatred in his heart even though he doesn't take revenge.

What Is Rashi Saying?

Taking revenge and bearing a grudge are not the same thing; they are two different commandments. Rashi clarifies the difference between taking revenge and bearing a grudge. He does this by means of two commonplace examples, which many of us may have experienced.

The meaning is clear. But if you look closely at Rashi's examples, you should have a question.

Your Question:

Questioning Rashi

A Question: Rashi gives two examples. In the first example A asks B for a **scythe**, is refused and the next day he is asked by B for an **ax**. Did you notice that the situation is exactly reversed in the second example (of bearing a grudge). Here A asks for an **ax**, is refused, then is asked for a **scythe**. The switch is almost unnoticeable, but it is there and cannot be ignored. Why does Rashi change the scenario in the two cases?

Hint: Think. Think logically. Is there any relevant difference between an ax and a scythe?

YOUR ANSWER:

UNDERSTANDING RASHI

An Answer: A scythe is a sharp instrument used for cutting wheat, an ax needn't be particularly sharp to be useful. Using a scythe could blunt its blade and cause some loss to its owner. Much less so in the case of an ax. With this in mind, let us look again at the examples Rashi cites.

In the first case (of revenge) *A* asks *B* to lend him his delicate scythe, he refused, conceivably because he was concerned not have its blade ruined. Next day *B* asks *A* if he can borrow his ax. If *A* refuses, it is clearly only because of his taking revenge, since an ax will not likely be dulled by a day's use. On the other hand, if the case were one where he was asked to lend his scythe and refused, we could not confidently ascribe this to the revenge motive. Maybe he just wanted to protect his valuable tool. Only refusal to lend an ax could make the point of revenge stick out.

In the second case (of bearing a grudge), *B* is asked to lend *A* an ax. He refuses (with less excuse of a loss since the ax is less likely to be ruined); the next day he asks *A* for a scythe and is given it! The owner could have justifiably refused, being concerned that its sharp blade might be damaged. Yet he lends it to his neighbor. As he does, he shows how he still bears a grudge, by comparing his generous behavior to his neighbor's stingy behavior. We could say his gratuitous comment ("I'm not like you") was meant to "turn the blade" on his neighbor's unneighborly behavior the day before! It clearly shows that he is bearing a grudge.

We see how each case was chosen to exemplify the most striking example to underline its message. The exquisite sensitivity of the Sages to the nuances of human emotions is shown by their deliberate choice of cases.

(See *Havanas Hamikra*)

Rashi deviates from his customary style in commentary, to make an important point.

Leviticus 19:18

לֹא־תִקֹּם וְלֹא־תִטֹּר אֶת־בְּנֵי עַמֶּךָ וְאָהַבְתָּ לְרֵעֲךָ כָּמוֹךָ אֲנִי ה'.

וְאָהַבְתָּ לְרֵעֲךָ כָּמוֹךָ. אמר רבי עקיבא: זה כלל גדול בתורה.
And you shall love your neighbor as yourself. *Rashi:*
Said Rabbi Akiva: This is a great principle in the Torah.

Rashi's *Midrashic* Source

Rashi's quote comes from the *midrash Toras Cohanim.* There is says:

" 'And you shall love your neighbor as yourself.' Rabbi Akiva said: This is a great principle in the Torah. Ben Azai said: 'This is the book of the generations of man.' (Genesis 5:1) This is an even greater principle."

From the *midrash* we see that Rabbi Akiva's opinion does not go unchallenged; Ben Azai has a different view. Rashi chooses Rabbi Akiva's view.

Rabbi Akiva probably derived his lesson from the famous case of Hillel the Elder which is recorded in tractate *Shabbos* 31a.

> "Once it happened that a gentile came to Shamai and said 'Convert me on the condition that you teach me the whole Torah while I stand on one foot.' He (Shamai) pushed him out with a builder's pole that was in his hand. He (the gentile) then went to Hillel. He (Hillel) converted him and said 'What you dislike, do not do to your friend. This is the whole Torah. The rest is commentary. Go and learn!' "

Hillel's principle, "What you dislike, don't do to your friend", is certainly the intention of our verse, only phrased in the negative. Hillel's phrase "This is the whole Torah" is similar to Rabbi Akiva's "This is a great principle in the Torah." Both of these giants of Talmudic teaching saw the essential core of the Torah to be the mitzvos between man and man. And by adding this comment to his commentary, we can add to that illustrious twosome, the name of Rashi as well.

Rashi's Unusual Use of *Midrash*

Rashi's comment here is quite unusual. No attempt to discover "What is bothering Rashi?" or "What misunderstanding is he warning us about?" can come up with any reasonable explanation for the need for Rashi's comment. We are left with one conclusion:

Rashi quoted Rabbi Akiva here, not because of the needs of Torah commentary, but because he too felt this to be a great principle of the Torah and he could not pass over it without pointing this out. Rashi, the Torah commentator, here becomes Rashi, the Living Torah teacher. One could say that Rashi reveals his true inner self here. He breaks with his custom of interpreting the words of the Torah, to tell us this great principle. As if to say: Learning Torah is an important and beloved activity, but don't lose sight of the ultimate principle — "Love your neighbor as yourself." Rashi's own life and conduct was a living example of this principle.

A DEEPER LOOK

Ben Azai Said "This is the Book of the generations of man..."

> Ben Azai's opinion is not at all clear. Why does he think that this innocent looking verse from Genesis teaches us a principle even greater than Rabbi Akiva's "Love thy neighbor" principle? The full verse reads:

> "This is the book of the generations of man, on the day that G-d created man, in the image of G-d He made him."

> What in that verse could possibly teach a principle greater than that of Rabbi Akiva?

YOUR ANSWER:

A DEEPER UNDERSTANDING

An Answer: The *Torah Temima* points out a deep insight here. Rabbi Akiva's principle (and that as explained by Hillel) is based on the assumption that each man loves himself. He is therefore commanded to love his neighbor *as himself*. But what of the depressed, self-hating or apathetic individual who couldn't care less about himself? He doesn't love anyone, not even himself. Such a person could reason that since I don't want anyone else's favors or kindness, I, therefore, have no obligation to be good or kind to others!

Therefore Ben Azai states that man's self-love is *not the measure of all things*. Man is made in the image of G-d, as this verse tells us. It is for this reason that he must respect and show kindness to other people, each of whom is made in the image of G-d. Ben Azai's principle is greater than that of Rabbi Akiva because it is the very foundation of "Love thy neighbor as thyself."

(See *Torah Temimah*)

**Parashas Emor is dedicated
in Memory of**

רות בן אהרן הכהן ע״ה
Ruth Koplowitz

and

מאיר בן קלמן ע״ה
Milton Klein

by their children
Robert and Hannah Klein
Silver Spring, MD

פרשת אמור

A close analysis of the Torah's words leads to an original interpretation.

Leviticus 21:1

וַיֹּאמֶר ה' אֶל־מֹשֶׁה אֱמֹר אֶל־הַכֹּהֲנִים בְּנֵי אַהֲרֹן וְאָמַרְתָּ אֲלֵהֶם
לְנֶפֶשׁ לֹא־יִטַּמָּא בְּעַמָּיו.

אמר אל הכהנים. אמר ואמרת להזהיר גדולים על הקטנים.
Say to the Priests: *Rashi*: 'Say' and 'and you shall say'
come to admonish the adults about their children [that
they too should avoid becoming unclean.]

WHAT IS RASHI SAYING?

Rashi tells us that adult priests must take care that their children, even minors, should not become defiled through contact with the dead.

What would you ask here?

YOUR QUESTION:

QUESTIONING RASHI

A Question: On what basis does Rashi (actually the Talmud *Yevomos* 114a) draw this conclusion?

What in the verse leads him to this?

YOUR ANSWER:

WHAT IS BOTHERING RASHI?

An Answer: As Rashi himself says, quoting the verse: "Say" and again "you shall say" is a very unusual construction. We frequently have "And

147 —

Moses *spoke*, וידבר, *saying*, לאמר." Or "*Speak* to the Children of Israel *saying*." In such cases "speak" is a general term while "say" means to convey a specific communication. But "Say" together with "you shall say" calls for an interpretation. How does Rashi's comment deal with this? Think this through.

YOUR ANSWER:

UNDERSTANDING RASHI

An Answer: The double "say" gives the verse a completely different meaning. G-d tells Moses: "Speak to the Priests [and when you speak to them, tell them] 'And you (individual priests) say to them (your children): do not defile yourselves.'"

This is certainly an original interpretation, because ordinarily we would assume that both "sayings" were addressed to the same group — adult priests. With Rashi's interpretation, only the first "saying" is addressed to the adult priest, while the second is addressed to the child priest.

But we can still ask:

How does Rashi know that the "them" refers to children, minors? Maybe it refers to other adults.

YOUR ANSWER:

A DEEPER UNDERSTANDING

An Answer: The word "them" cannot refer to other adult priests because whenever Moses speaks to the people he addresses all adult males; they needn't receive the communication via someone else. So if the adult priest is commanded to tell this *mitzvah* to another priest, it must perforce be to a minor priest who is ordinarily not commanded directly by Moses.

Because of his position in Israel's society and his obligations in the Temple, the priest had to take more stringent measures to insure his ritual purity. Therefore even his young children must be careful in this respect, although this is not a bonafide *mitzvah*.

(See *Mizrachi*)

Rashi gives us a lesson in Talmudic reasoning.

Leviticus 21:1 (Same verse as above.)

וַיֹּאמֶר הי אֶל־מֹשֶׁה אֱמֹר אֶל־הַכֹּהֲנִים בְּנֵי אַהֲרֹן וְאָמַרְתָּ אֲלֵהֶם לְנֶפֶשׁ לֹא־יִטַּמָּא בְּעַמָּיו.

בני אהרן. יכול חללים, תלמוד לומר "הכהנים."

בני אהרן. אף בעלי מומין במשמע.

בני אהרן. ולא בנות אהרן.

The sons of Aaron: *Rashi*: Perhaps also those unfit to serve (*challalim*) may also not defile themselves, therefore it says "[only] the priests."
The sons of Aaron: *Rashi*: Also those with bodily blemishes are intended.
The sons of Aaron: *Rashi*: But not the daughters of Aaron.

WHAT IS RASHI SAYING?

Rashi lists those of the children of Aaron who are included in the laws of priestly purity and impurity. The priest is forbidden to come in contact with a dead body, except for the seven relatives mentioned. Rashi teaches us that these laws apply to some but not to others in the priestly family. *Challalim* (those born of a marriage which is forbidden to priests) are not included. On the other hand, priests who have bodily blemishes, which ordinarily prohibits them from serving in the Temple, are nevertheless included in these prohibitions. Daughters of priests, on the other hand, are excluded.

The comment is tricky because it includes and excludes people apparently on the basis of the very same words — בני אהרן. Let us see if we can understand the logic behind these interpretive rules. But first, we must question the comment as a whole.

What would you ask?

YOUR QUESTION:

QUESTIONING RASHI

A Question: Why are there any legal interpretations (*drashos*) here at all? What about the verse makes them necessary?

What is bothering Rashi?

Hint: Compare our verse with verses 2:2 and 3:2.

YOUR ANSWER:

What Is Bothering Rashi?

An Answer:　See the words הכהנים בני אהרן "the priests, the sons of Aaron." There is a redundancy here. Priests are by definition the sons of Aaron, you cannot be a priest without being a son of Aaron. So the words "sons of Aaron" are unnecessary. Did you notice the order of the words in the two verses cited above? There it says בני אהרן הכהנים "the sons of Aaron, the priests." This is reasonable and not redundant, because the word "priests" tells us which of Aaron's sons the Torah is referring to, since not all of Aaron's sons may be priests. But the order in our verse makes the words "the sons of Aaron" clearly unnecessary. Why the double term? This is what is bothering Rashi. The *drashos* are based on this redundancy.

But how is it that Rashi comments three times on the same words — בני אהרן? And how is it that these words exclude certain people (*challalim*, and women) and these same words include people (a blemished priest)? It looks quite arbitrary. Can you find any method to the *drashos*? Here we have a perfect example of Talmudic reasoning.

Think.

YOUR ANSWER:

Understanding Rashi

An Answer: Let us take this slowly, logical step by logical step, so that each step (and there are several) can be digested mentally.

　　　* The words בני אהרן are a broad, inclusive term, which can include all of Aaron's children. The word כהנים is a narrower, more re-strictive term, which reasonably includes only those fit to do serv-ice in the Temple.

　　　* The two terms are in opposition, they thereby create a tension be-tween them, each pulling in opposite directions — excluding and including people into the category of people who are commanded to observe the laws of priestly purity.

Now let us look at the reasoning.

First Rashi says:

> * **The sons of Aaron**: *Rashi*: Perhaps also those unfit to serve (*challalim*) may also not defile themselves, therefore it says "[only] the priests."

Rashi is saying that the "sons of Aaron" is an inclusive term, so maybe it includes even *challalim* ? No, says Rashi, that is why we have the term "the priests," in order to exclude them, since we know that *challalim* cannot act in the priestly capacity.

Rashi continues:

> * **The sons of Aaron**: *Rashi*: Also those with bodily blemishes are intended.

Rashi seems to say that the inclusive term "sons of Aaron" includes those with blemishes. But why doesn't Rashi exclude these people by saying "therefore it says '[only] the priests' which should exclude those with blemishes. He used this kind of logic above, why not here as well?

Hint: See the verses further on which speak of the laws of priests with blemishes (21:17-23).

YOUR ANSWER:

An Answer: The Torah says explicitly (21:21,22) that one with a blemish may not serve in the Temple but may eat of the sacrifices.:

> "Any man from the offspring of Aaron, the Priest, that has a blemish shall not come near to offer a fire-offering of *Hashem*; he has a blemish, the food of his G-d he shall not come near to offer. *The food of his G-d of the holy of holies and the holies he may eat.*"

Now we can understand why Rashi didn't exclude the blemished priests, because the Torah explicitly allows them to partake of the sacrifices (which a *challal* can't). In this way the Torah accords them some level of priesthood. Note Rashi's precise phrasing here. He does not say that the words בני אהרן are necessary to include the blemished. He says rather "also those with blemishes are intended" meaning that elsewhere the Torah includes them. By including those with blemishes by the explicit Torah verse and not by use of the words בני אהרן, this leaves the words בני אהרן open for a further *drasha*. These words are now free to exclude the daughters of Aaron — the sons of Aaron and not the daughters of Aaron. It should be said that the words בני אהרן may mean the "sons of

Aaron" or the "children of Aaron." We know that the term בני ישראל includes all Israelites not just the men. So why should we interpret the words בני אהרן narrowly and exclude women?

The answer is that the words בני אהרן are redundant, it would be sufficient to say just הכהנים. The addition of these words indicates that they teach us something: בני אהרן ולא בנות אהרן.

* To review: the word כהנים is necessary to exclude *challalim*. But why do we need the words בני אהרן, the word כהנים is sufficient to teach this.

* Rashi gives us the answer; when he adds that the words בני אהרן are necessary in order to exclude women from the service and from the laws of priestly purity.

In Summary: The two similar, but opposing, terms each have their respective functions, one to include, the other to exclude, as the case may be. Keep in mind that the words בני אהרן are not the source for including the blemished priest, the Torah explicitly included them. Rashi's comments and the precise way he phrases them, shows that no word is extra, no word is without its unique lesson.

(See *Mizrachi, Silbermann*)

This comment illustrates, among other things, the importance of Rashi's dibbur hamaschil.

Leviticus 23:2

דַּבֵּר אֶל־בְּנֵי יִשְׂרָאֵל וְאָמַרְתָּ אֲלֵהֶם מוֹעֲדֵי ה' אֲשֶׁר תִּקְרְאוּ אֹתָם מִקְרָאֵי קֹדֶשׁ אֵלֶּה הֵם מוֹעֲדָי.

דַּבֵּר אֶל בְּנֵי יִשְׂרָאֵל... מוֹעֲדֵי ה'. עשה מועדות שיהיו ישראל מלומדין בהם, שמעבירים את השנה על גלויות שנעקרו ממקומן לעלות לרגל, ועדיין לא הגיעו לירושלים.

Speak to the Children of Israel.... G-d's appointed times. *Rashi*: Regulate the appointed times so that [all] Israel can [participate] in them. This teaches us that they proclaim a leap year because of the exiles who have left their homes to ascend for the festival but have not yet arrived in Jerusalem.

BACKGROUND

During the Temple period it was a *mitzvah* to make a pilgrimage to Jerusalem for the festivals in order to participate in the Temple service. During the Second Temple many Jews remained in exile, many in Babylon and some in Egypt. The trip to Jerusalem was long and particularly difficult if the roads were muddied by the rains. Therefore if the Festival of Passover fell out early in the year, while the rains were still falling, the pilgrims would most likely be delayed. Therefore, the Sanhedrin, who had the power to proclaim a leap year by adding a second Adar, would do so in order to push Passover off until after the rainy season, so that they would arrive in time for the Festival. This is what Rashi says our verse teaches us.

What would you ask about the comment?

YOUR QUESTION:

QUESTIONING RASHI

A Question: How does Rashi find this in the Torah's words?

This is not easy. Perhaps you can get it.

Hint: Look closely at the *dibbur hamaschil.*

YOUR ANSWER:

WHAT IS BOTHERING RASHI?

An Answer: The verse says "Speak to the *Children of Israel*" to declare the Holy days; but it is not the people who make this declaration; it is the Elders, the Sanhedrin. So the words "Speak to the Children of Israel" must have a different message.

Now, notice what Rashi does. Look at his *dibbur hamaschil.*

Do you see anything unusual?

YOUR ANSWER:

Rashi's *Dibbur Hamaschil*

Answer: Rashi deletes the words "and say to them" in order to place the words "Children of Israel" immediately next to the words "G-d's Appointed Times." This is certainly intentional and the idea is derived from the *midrash Toras Cohanim*.

Rashi's *Midrashic* Source

There the *midrash* says:

"How do we learn that we proclaim a leap year for the exiles who have left home but have not yet arrived in Jerusalem? Because it says '**Children of Israel...G-d's Appointed Times**.' Make the Appointed Times so that *all* Israel can participate."

We see that Rashi makes the connection as the *midrash* does; Rashi does this by his abbreviated *dibbur hamaschil*.

The Significance of the People's Participation

It is obvious that it is important to have the people participate in these national/religious Holy days. But it is not as obvious why the Sanhedrin went through all this effort so that each and every Jew, even those in exile, could attend.

I would suggest that a nuance in the words of our verse may hint at the significance of the personal participation of each Jew at these festivals.

Do you see anything unusual about the wording?

Your Answer:

A Deeper Understanding

An Answer: Notice that the verse begins with the words "*G-d's* Appointed Times" and ends with G-d saying "these are *My* Appointed Times." The switch from the impersonal, third person ("G-d's") to the more personal, second person ("My") (as is the formula for our daily blessings), hints at the importance of meeting G-d personally. The Holy days and the Temple service are an appropriate vehicle for such a meeting. As it says in Deuteronomy 16:16 "Three times a year shall all your males appear before *Hashem*, your G-d, in the place He shall choose; on the Festival of Matzos, and on the Festival of Shavuoth and on the Festival of Succoth, and he shall not appear before *Hashem* empty-handed." And in a similar context, it says in Exodus 23:15 "they shall not *see My face* empty-handed." "Seeing My face" is certainly a vivid way of describing a personal encounter with *Hashem*. Perhaps it is for this reason that the Sanhedrin went to such lengths to enable each and every Jew to personally experience this Divine encounter.

A series of Rashi-comments that grapple with understanding a difficulty in the Torah by means of both p'shat and drash.

Leviticus 23:16

עַד מִמָּחֳרַת הַשַּׁבָּת הַשְּׁבִיעִת תִּסְפְּרוּ חֲמִשִּׁים יוֹם וְהִקְרַבְתֶּם מִנְחָה חֲדָשָׁה לַה'.

"Until the morrow of the seventh week you shall count fifty days and you shall bring a new meal offering to *Hashem*."

עד ממחרת השבת השביעת תספרו. ולא עד בכלל, והן ארבעים ותשעה יום.

חמשים יום והקרבתם מנחה חדשה לה'. ביום החמשים תקריבוה, ואומר אני זה מדרשו אבל פשוטו עד ממחרת השבת השביעית שהוא יום חמשים תספרו, ומקרא מסורס הוא.

Until the morrow of the seventh week: *Rashi*: [Until,] but not including [the fiftieth day] and they are, thus, forty-nine days.

Fifty days and you shall bring a new meal offering to Hashem: *Rashi*: On the fiftieth day you shall bring it. I say this is the *midrashic* interpretation. But its *p'shat* is: Until the morrow of the seventh week — which is the fiftieth day — you shall count. This is an inverted verse."

WHAT IS RASHI SAYING? _____

Rashi breaks up the verse in an unusual way and offers two comments. In the first comment, he says that although the verse seems to say we are to count 50 days, in actuality the verse means we are to count only 49 days.

In the second comment, he offers two interpretations. The first he labels as *midrash*, the second as *p'shat*. It is not readily apparent why one is more *drash* than the other, since neither interpretation takes the verse as it is ordinarily translated (see our translation of the verse above).

Nevertheless, both interpretations come to answer Rashi's implicit question.

What is it?

Hint: Look at the previous verse and compare it to ours.

What's bothering Rashi?

YOUR ANSWER:

WHAT IS BOTHERING RASHI ? _____

An Answer: The previous verse says "You shall count for yourselves — from the morrow of the rest day (Pesach), from the day on which you will bring the *omer* wave-offering — seven weeks; they shall be complete." Seven weeks is seven times seven days which equals 49 days. Yet our verse says "Until the morrow of the seventh week you shall count fifty days ..." A blatant contradiction. How can these two contradictory verses be reconciled?

This is what is bothering Rashi.

How do his interpretations answer this problem?

Hint: Look closely at his *dibbur hamaschil* and compare these words with those in the Torah verse.

YOUR ANSWER:

UNDERSTANDING RASHI _____

An Answer: In the Torah, the *esnachta* (comma) is under the word "day," meaning this is a stop. With this in mind, the verse reads: "Until the morrow of the seventh week count *fifty* days. [new sentence] And you shall bring a new meal-offering to *Hashem*." Thus, the word חמשים is a cardinal number (fifty). However Rashi breaks up the verse differently, he puts the comma earlier, under the word "you shall count." According to Rashi, both in *drash* and *p'shat*, the word חמשים is an ordinal number (fiftieth). The verse now reads according to the *drash*: "Up until the morrow of the seventh week count. [new sentence] On the fiftieth day bring a new meal-offering to *Hashem*." Now there is no contradiction. Both verse 15 and our verse 16, mean we are to count only 49 days, then on the fiftieth day we are to offer the new offering.

"But Its *P'shat* Is"

After the *midrashic* interpretation, Rashi offers what he considers to be the *p'shat* interpretation. As opposed to the *midrash*, his *p'shat* interpretation puts the words "fiftieth day" together with the first part of the verse: "Until the morrow of the seventh week — which is the fiftieth day — [then] you shall bring a new meal-offering."

Note that these interpretations in Rashi, both the *drash* and the *p'shat*, while they differ as to where they place the comma, both translate חמשים יום as "fiftieth day." This avoids the contradiction that would have existed were the word translated as "fifty days."

P'shat and *Drash* in Rashi

It remains to be understood why, in Rashi's eyes, one of these interpretations is *p'shat* and one is *drash*, since neither interprets the verse the way it is simply translated, i.e. "...count fifty days. And you shall bring..."

Can you differentiate between *p'shat* and *drash* here?

Your Answer:

An Answer: In both interpretations, Rashi introduces changes in the text. Let us compare these changes and see if we can determine the difference between *p'shat* and *drash* in this way.

Drash:

1) Fifty days is connected with the second half of the verse (ignoring the *esnachta*)

2) חמשים יום is reversed to ביום החמשים

P'shat:

1) Fifty days is connected with the first part of the verse (in accordance with the *esnachta*)

2) חמשים יום is reversed to יום חמשים

3) תספרו חמשים יום is reversed to יום חמשים תספרו (This is what Rashi calls an "inverted verse".)

Can you see now why one is considered *p'shat*, the other *drash*?

YOUR ANSWER:

UNDERSTANDING *P'SHAT* AND *DRASH*

An Answer: In both interpretations, words are reversed. So this is not a difference. The main difference is that one interprets the verse according to the musical notes (called *trop*), the *esnachta*, and one ignores the *esnachta*. Rashi is telling us that *p'shat* must fit in with the musical notes; if it doesn't, the interpretation must be considered *drash*.

"I SAY THIS IS THE *MIDRASHIC* INTERPRETATION"

This is a strange statement. What does Rashi mean "I say this is a *midrash*"? Either it is or it is not a *midrash*! It is not up to Rashi to determine if this interpretation is a *midrash*. Rashi's *midrashic* sources for his commentary on Leviticus are generally one of the following: The *midrash-halacha Toras Cohanim*; the *midrash-haggada Vayikra Rabbah* or the Talmud. When Rashi quotes a *midrash*, he certainly knows where he found it. Why then does he say "I say this is a *midrash*"?

But, lo and behold, Rashi's first interpretation, which he calls *midrashic*, is not found anywhere in the *midrash*! (This can be checked by using Rabbi Menachem Kasher's encyclopedia *Torah Shelaimah*; this *midrash* is not cited there.) It would appear to be Rashi's own interpretation or one he received from his teachers.

An IMPORTANT LESSON

If Rashi is not citing a *midrash*, why does he call it a *midrash*? The answer is that the term *midrash* refers to a mode of interpretation, which is not *p'shat*. Rashi is saying that this interpretation (the one that ignores the *esnachta*) is a *midrash*-type interpretation — even though it is not one of the recorded *midrashim* of the Sages. And as we pointed out above, Rashi calls the interpretation that does follow the musical notes, *p'shat*.

"A Reversed Verse"

In Hebrew the term is "*mikra mesuras*" which means literally a "castrated verse." It can mean either a verse that leaves out a word, usually one that is self-understood, or a verse that has some words reversed, as in our case. The "*mikra mesuras*" is used frequently in the Torah. Because of its frequency, Rashi does not consider this to be sufficient reason to consider such a verse as non-*p'shat*.

(See *Mizrachi*)

Rashi abandons p'shat to teach a lesson. The Ramban has a different view.

Leviticus 23:24

דַּבֵּר אֶל־בְּנֵי יִשְׂרָאֵל לֵאמֹר בַּחֹדֶשׁ הַשְּׁבִיעִי בְּאֶחָד לַחֹדֶשׁ יִהְיֶה לָכֶם שַׁבָּתוֹן זִכְרוֹן תְּרוּעָה מִקְרָא קֹדֶשׁ.

זכרון תרועה. זכרון פסוקי זכרונות ופסוקי שופרות. לזכור לכם עקידת יצחק שקרב תחתיו איל.

A remembrance with shofar blasts. *Rashi*: A remembrance by means of Biblical verses which treat of the Divine remembrance and which have reference to the blowing of the shofar (ram's horn); that I may recall to memory for your sake the *akaidah* of Isaac in whose stead a ram was offered.

What would you ask here?

YOUR QUESTION:

QUESTIONING RASHI

A Question: How does Rashi derive this from our verse?

Is something problematic here?

YOUR ANSWER:

WHAT IS BOTHERING RASHI?

An Answer: Some suggest (the *Sifsei Chachomim*) that Rashi was bothered by the discrepancy between this verse and the verse in Numbers 29:1. There it says:

וּבַחֹדֶשׁ הַשְּׁבִיעִי בְּאֶחָד לַחֹדֶשׁ מִקְרָא־קֹדֶשׁ יִהְיֶה לָכֶם כָּל־מְלֶאכֶת עֲבֹדָה לֹא תַעֲשׂוּ יוֹם תְּרוּעָה יִהְיֶה לָכֶם.

In Numbers 29:1, Rosh Hashana is called יום תרועה "a day of [shofar] sounding." Why then does our verse call the very same day "a day of remembering the [shofar] sounding"? Why the difference? This, says the *Sifsei Chachomim*, is what is bothering Rashi.

The difference between these two verses does raise a problem (the Sages asked about this in the tractate *Rosh Hashana* 29b.) But it is difficult to accept that this is what was bothering Rashi. Because it is not Rashi's style to ask a question based on information which appears later in the Torah. Rashi wrote his commentary to deal with questions that might arise as we read the Torah in sequence. If this were the basis for Rashi's comment, we would expect him to make this comment in Numbers 29:1 where the contradiction is fully exposed.

We must look elsewhere for understanding what's bothering him.

The answer may be much simpler.

YOUR ANSWER:

WHAT IS REALLY BOTHERING RASHI?

An Answer: The words זכרון תרועה are strange. A תרועה is a blowing of the shofar. But what could זכרון תרועה "remembrance of a blowing" possibly mean?

This, in all likelihood, is what Rashi is reacting to.

We can see that his comment is meant to make sense out of these words זכרון תרועה.

He tells us that the remembrance mentioned here refers to the inclusion of these verses in our prayers of Rosh Hashana.

But if that is the meaning of these words, then it leads to another question.

Can you think of it?

YOUR QUESTION:

Some history may be of help.

SOME HISTORICAL BACKGROUND

The Men of the Great Assembly (post-biblical and pre-talmudic era) instituted our formalized prayers. They organized the prayers for Rosh Hashana around three themes: *Shofaros*/Ram's horn; *Malchyos*/G-d's Kingship and *Zichronos*/G-d's Remembrances. For each of these themes, ten verses from the Scriptures are recited in the Amidah prayer. These are the verses that Rashi is referring to.

Knowing that, what would you ask on his comment?

YOUR QUESTION:

THE RAMBAN QUESTIONS RASHI

A Question: The Ramban asks an obvious question. How does the Biblical verse refer to rules and regulations (the formal prayers) that were only instituted centuries later? To put it in more legal terminology: These prayers are of Rabbinical origination, and not a Biblical law. How, then, can Rashi say that the Torah verse refers to them?

The fact that the recitation of these verses is of Rabbinical (and not of Mosaic) origin was certainly known to Rashi. Why then did he explain the Torah's words in this way? This is a super-question. There does not seem to be any way around it.

I would suggest an answer that gives us an insight about Rashi's exegetical style.

UNDERSTANDING RASHI'S STYLE

Rashi never made explicit all his goals in commentary. But we can speculate. From the variety of his comments we can say that his Torah commentary has several goals. One, of course, is to explain the verses according to *p'shat*. But we have seen that he has other purposes as well. He uses *midrash* often to inspire, as we saw by his opening comment to the Book of Leviticus. (See our discussion there.) His commentary also includes many moral teachings, and they are not necessarily bound to a *p'shat* interpretation. Another goal may be to show the layman the foundations of his daily religious practice. All Jews were familiar with the High holiday prayers, and with their threefold message. Rashi's comment here, while not being accurate from a *p'shat* perspective, was enlightening from a total Torah/Talmudic perspective. It has the effect of anchoring a familiar custom in the Torah's words. This is a known Talmudical method, and is called an *asamachta*, meaning a Biblical textual support for a Rabbinical law. If the Talmud did, it is good enough for Rashi!

But if Rashi is not giving us *p'shat*, what might be the *p'shat* interpretation of the strange words זכרון תרועה ?

The Ramban analyzes this verse from several angles, among them is his *p'shat* understanding.

THE RAMBAN'S *P'SHAT* INTERPRETATION

"Rather the expression זכרון תרועה is like the verse יום תרועה יהיה לכם.
[Note: He sees no conflict between the two verses on a *p'shat* level.]
Scripture states that we are to blow on that day and this shall be for us *a memorial before G-d*. As it says further on, 'and you shall blow the trumpets and they shall be for you *a memorial before your G-d*.' (Numbers 10:10)"

The Ramban is saying that the purpose of the sounding of the shofar is so that we will be remembered by G-d and our prayers answered. Other interpretations of the shofar blast have been given, such as "wake up you sleepers, " this being a call to teshuva. Or trumpeting the King's presence. But none of these meanings accords with use of the word זכרון in our verse, as does the Ramban's *p'shat*.

(See *Ramban, Sefer Zikaron*)

Rashi chooses the supernatural midrash over the natural in order to give us p'shat.

Leviticus 23:43

לְמַעַן יֵדְעוּ דֹרֹתֵיכֶם כִּי בַסֻּכּוֹת הוֹשַׁבְתִּי אֶת־בְּנֵי יִשְׂרָאֵל בְּהוֹצִיאִי
אוֹתָם מֵאֶרֶץ מִצְרָיִם אֲנִי הי אֱלֹקֵיכֶם.

כי בסכת הושבתי. ענני כבוד.
Because in booths I caused [the Children of Israel] to dwell. *Rashi*: [In] Clouds of glory.

RASHI'S MIDRASHIC SOURCE

The source of the comment is the Talmud tractate *Succa* 11b.

There we find the following dispute:

"Because in booths I caused the Children of Israel to dwell." These were Clouds of Glory, such is the opinion of Rabbi Eliezer. Rabbi Akiva said "Actual *succoth* He made for them ."

QUESTIONING RASHI

Of the two opinions, Rashi has chosen Rabbi Eliezer's. Of these two opinions, Rabbi Akiva's is the more natural one, that the *succoth* mentioned in this verse were real *succoth* of wood and having a roof of vegetation.

Why would Rashi choose the supernatural interpretation of Rabbi Eliezer over the natural one of Rabbi Akiva?

What in the verse led him to this choice?

Hint: Look closely at the *dibbur hamaschil*.

YOUR ANSWER:

UNDERSTANDING RASHI

An Answer: The Torah's words are הושבתי את בני ישראל "I made dwell." If the Torah were speaking of normal *succoth* then it should have said: "Because the Children of Israel dwelt in *succoth*." The wording as we have it clearly implies that G-d *made them dwell* in the *succoth*, this can best be explained if He made Clouds of Glory and encompassed them inside.

A Lesson

We see that *p'shat*, which is always in accordance with the words of the Torah, need not necessarily prefere a natural description of events. The supernatural is inherent in the Torah and interpreting a verse in such a way is "natural" and may well be *p'shat*. (See a similar interpretation by Rashi of Genesis 32:3.)

A brilliant interpretation by the Lubavitcher Rebbi clarifies a puzzling Rashi-comment.

Leviticus 24:14

הוֹצֵא אֶת־הַמְקַלֵּל אֶל־מִחוּץ לַמַּחֲנֶה וְסָמְכוּ כָל־הַשֹּׁמְעִים אֶת־יְדֵיהֶם
עַל־רֹאשׁוֹ וְרָגְמוּ אֹתוֹ כָּל־הָעֵדָה.

אֶת יְדֵיהֶם [עַל רֹאשׁוֹ]. אוֹמְרִים לוֹ. דָּמְךָ בְּרֹאשְׁךָ וְאֵין אָנוּ נֶעֱנָשִׁים
בְּמִיתָתְךָ, שֶׁאַתָּה גָּרַמְתָּ לָךְ.

Their hands [on his head]: *Rashi:* They said to him: your blood is on your own head, we will not be punished for your death, for it was you, yourself, who brought this about.

Your Question:

Questioning Rashi

A Question: Why the need to apologize? If the man is guilty and should be put to death, why do the executioners need to plead innocence? In no other death sentence do we find such a statement. Why here?

Can you explain this? What brought Rashi to assume the necessity for such a statement on behalf of the executioners?

Hint: Compare our verse with other cases of stoning executions. Some examples: Leviticus 20:2; 20:27; Deut. 21:21; 22:24.

What's bothering Rashi here?

Your Answer:

WHAT IS BOTHERING RASHI?

An Answer: Did you make an amazing discovery? You should have! In each and every case of stoning in the Torah, the stoning is mentioned together with "and he shall certainly die" or some similar statement of death. Only in our verse and in verse 24:23 where the implementation of this punishment is described, is *no mention made of death*! Such a deviation from such an encompassing consistency is no accident.

How would you understand it?

YOUR ANSWER:

UNDERSTANDING RASHI

An Answer: The Lubavitcher Rebbe concludes from this that this man was not sentenced to death, since no mention of death is found here. He was sentenced to be stoned, perhaps just once. And while this probably would not kill him, it might. Thus Rashi's comment.

These "executioners" are to place their hands on his head to symbolize their message: Your own blood is on your head, for if, by chance, you die from our one-time stoning, you alone are to blame. Because if you do die, then certainly G-d had a part in your death. It was His (not ours) way of punishing you for your deed."

That is why here, and only here, of all the cases of stoning in the Torah, is this apology necessary and relevant.

But, if this is so, then you should have a question on this.

YOUR QUESTION:

A DEEPER QUESTION

A Question: Why was he not sentenced to death? Why is this an exception to the rule that stoning is always a capital punishment?

Hint: Is there anything unusual about this case?

YOUR ANSWER:

A Deeper Understanding

An Answer: This man was convicted of a crime without knowing what punishment he deserved. Even Moses did not know the appropriate punishment (see verse 13). According to Biblical law one must always be warned first. He must be informed of the punishment he will receive if he should violate the law. This man was not given a fair warning, thus he could not fairly receive a death punishment. It was a special case called in Hebrew הוראת שעה that he was punished at all. But his punishment was only to be symbolic, a one-time stoning. This is why here, and here only, death was not the requisite punishment.

Lesson

One marvels at the subtleties in the Torah. Subtleties that can go unnoticed for generations...until one takes a closer look at the familiar words of the Torah.... with the help of Rashi.

(See M.M. Shneerson, *Bi'urim L'pirush Rashi*)

פרשת בהר

Rashi veers from p'shat to teach us a Rabbinical law. The Ramban differs.

Leviticus 25:9

וְהַעֲבַרְתָּ שׁוֹפַר תְּרוּעָה בַּחֹדֶשׁ הַשְּׁבִעִי בֶּעָשׂוֹר לַחֹדֶשׁ בְּיוֹם הַכִּפֻּרִים תַּעֲבִירוּ שׁוֹפָר בְּכָל־אַרְצְכֶם.

בְּיוֹם הַכִּפּוּרִים. ממשמע שנאמר ביום הכפורים, איני יודע שהוא בעשור לחודש? אם כן למה נאמר בעשור לחדש? אלא לומר לך תקיעה בעשור לחדש דוחה שבת בכל ארצכם ואין תקיעת ראש השנה דוחה שבת בכל ארצכם אלא בבית דין בלבד.

On Yom Kippur: *Rashi:* Since it said "on Yom Kippur" don't I know that it is on the tenth of the month? So why does it say "on the tenth of the month"? Rather, it is to tell you that blowing (the shofar) on the tenth of the month supersedes the Sabbath in all your land, but blowing (the shofar) on Rosh Hashanah does not supersede the Sabbath in all your land, only in the rabbinical court exclusively.

WHAT IS RASHI SAYING?

Rashi cites an halachic law permitting the blowing the shofar on Yom Kippur (which occurs only on the Jubilee year) when it falls out on the Sabbath. This is based on a classic *midrashic* principle, i.e, that new laws are derived from the Torah from redundant words and phrases. In our verse there is a redundancy. It says both "on the tenth day of the seventh month" as well as "on Yom Kippur." These are the same day, why the duplication? This is what is bothering the *midrash* and, in turn, what is bothering Rashi. But the use of that method here is strange.

Do you see something unusual about the question of duplication here?

What would you ask about it?

Your Question:

Questioning Rashi _____

A Question: The verse says: "You shall blow the shofar on the tenth of the seventh month, on the Yom Kippur ..." Since both the "tenth of the
seventh month" and "Yom Kippur" designate the same day, which
of these terms would you say is redundant in this verse?

Logic would dictate that the words "Yom Kippur" are unnecessary because the Torah has just said "the tenth of the seventh month" which is
Yom Kippur! The unnecessary words are always those that come second, not those that come first; in our case the words "Yom Kippur" come
second and thus are redundant. But Rashi says just the opposite; he says
that the words "tenth of the month" are redundant. It is not easy to understand why this switch is made.

Can you think of an answer?

Your Answer:

Understanding Rashi _____

An Answer: An answer suggested (*Mizrachi*) is that Rashi wants to emphasize
the difference between Yom Kippur and Rosh Hashanah. We know
that Yom Kippur has two designations in the Torah: "Yom Kippur"
and "the tenth of the seventh month." Rosh Hashanah, on the other
hand, has only one designation in the Torah: "the first of the seventh month." (Numbers 29:1) (Believe it or not the term "Rosh
Hashanah" does not appear in the Torah.) Therefore in order to
make the contrast more obvious, Rashi shows that the words "the
tenth of the month" are the extra ones so we can easily make the
deduction: "*tenth* of the seventh month" but not "*first* of the seventh month."

The Ramban's Comment on Rashi_____

Rashi's comment is somewhat misleading, as the Ramban points out:

"Now the Rav (Rashi) with his expert knowledge of the Talmud
and because it is all before him as an arranged table was not concerned when he quoted a *Beraisah* without qualification. But they

are misleading for the rest of the people (who are not as expert in the Talmud as he was). For it is known and clear in the Gemorah that all soundings of the shofar whether on the New Year or the Day of Atonement (in the Jubilee year) or even (sounding the shofar) out of one's desire (not for a *mitzvah*) are permitted on the Sabbath, since blowing (the shofar) is merely an art and not work..."

The Ramban goes on to show that the prohibition of blowing the shofar on the Sabbath is a merely a Rabbinical law but is not forbidden by the Torah. So the *drash* in our verse that the shofar is prohibited on the Sabbath, cannot be the actual meaning of the Torah's words. The Ramban is critical of Rashi because, he says, anyone not knowing the Rabbinical basis for this law would be mislead by Rashi and think that this is a Torah prohibition.

The Ramban shows great respect for Rashi. While he disagrees with Rashi's interpretation, he does not for a moment assume that Rashi was unaware of the Talmudic passage which states that blowing of the shofar is not considered "work" and thus is not prohibited on the Sabbath. (How could Rashi be unaware of it? He wrote a commentary on that tractate!) Yet, says the Ramban, Rashi wrote this comment in order to convey the importance of blowing the shofar "throughout the land" i.e., that every individual must hear it when it is blown on Yom Kippur.

To summarize the difficulty: Rashi's comment seems to say that the extra words in this verse teach us that we may not blow the shofar on Rosh Hashanah when it falls out on the Sabbath but we may do so when the Jubilee Yom Kippur falls out on the Sabbath. Yet these laws are known to be of Rabbinical origin and are not derived from the words of the Torah.

Can you defend Rashi? This certainly is not easy.

YOUR ANSWER:

In Defense of Rashi — Understanding His Style _____

An Answer: We must try to understand Rashi's style of interpretation in order to understand what he has done here. We have pointed out elsewhere (the Shemos volume of *"What's Bothering Rashi?"*, p.125) that Rashi sees *p'shat* through the eyes of the Sages. This may not always coincide with what we might consider the simple meaning of a verse. In our verse there is a clear difficulty, that is the redundancy of the words "tenth of the month" and "Yom Kippur." It is this redundancy that Rashi sets out to explain.

As we look closely at the verse, the redundancy stands out clearer.

The verse is constructed of two halves:

וְהַעֲבַרְתָּ שׁוֹפַר תְּרוּעָה בַּחֹדֶשׁ הַשְּׁבִעִי בֶּעָשׂוֹר לַחֹדֶשׁ

בְּיוֹם הַכִּפֻּרִים תַּעֲבִירוּ שׁוֹפָר בְּכָל־אַרְצְכֶם.

The halves look identical in meaning — except that the second adds the words "in all your land" and these words are placed together with "on Yom Kippur."

In view of this, Rashi wanted to explain the significance of the words "in all your land" in reference to Yom Kippur, words which do not appear in reference to Rosh Hashanah. In order to do so he made use of the Sage's *drash* — which said that the shofar is sounded on Yom Kippur/Sabbath but not on Rosh Hashanah/Sabbath. This *drash* shows the relative importance of the shofar on the Jubilee Yom Kippur over that of Rosh Hashanah.

THE LESSONS

Several things about Rashi's style can be learned from this comment.

* Rashi's Torah commentary does not necessary reflect the law as it is. Such is not the purpose in his commentary; its purpose being to explain difficulties in the text.

* Rashi, at times, will make use of the Sages' *drash* interpretations to explain difficulties on a *p'shat* level.

* Since Rashi wrote a comprehensive commentary on nearly all of the Babylonian Talmud, it is more than reasonable to assume that he knew its contents. The Ramban made this assumption about Rashi's knowledge and when he criticized him, he did so with caution and with all due respect. Therefore, whenever we are confronted with a contradiction between Rashi's Torah commentary and something in the Talmud we must diligently search for a solution that will reconcile the matter and not brush it off as due to Rashi's lack of knowledge or forgetfulness.

(See *Ramban*)

Rashi extracts the basic meaning of the Torah's words.

Leviticus 25:10

וְקִדַּשְׁתֶּם אֵת שְׁנַת הַחֲמִשִּׁים שָׁנָה וּקְרָאתֶם דְּרוֹר בָּאָרֶץ לְכָל־יֹשְׁבֶיהָ
יוֹבֵל הִוא תִּהְיֶה לָכֶם וְשַׁבְתֶּם אִישׁ אֶל־אֲחֻזָּתוֹ וְאִישׁ אֶל־מִשְׁפַּחְתּוֹ
תָּשֻׁבוּ.

וְשַׁבְתֶּם אִישׁ אֶל אֲחֻזָּתוֹ. שהשדות חוזרות לבעליהן.
And you shall return, every man to his heritage: *Rashi:*
That the fields return to their owners.

SOME BACKGROUND

This section deals with the laws of the Jubilee year. If a man sells his field, its ownership reverts back to him automatically on the fiftieth year, the Jubilee. Another law in the *parasha* (verses 25: 39ff) teaches us that if a man is sold into slavery he is freed in the Jubilee year, and he returns to his family.

As you look at our verse and Rashi's comment, what would you ask?

YOUR QUESTION:

QUESTIONING RASHI

A Question: The verse says that the owners return to their heritage; but Rashi says the fields return to their owner! This is the same thing, but phrased in other words. Why does Rashi rephrase and reverse the sentence in this way?

What is bothering him?

Hint: A subtle point.

YOUR ANSWER:

WHAT IS BOTHERING RASHI?

An Answer: This is a case of man selling his field. The verse says "You shall return, each man to his heritage..." Is that what actually happens? Does a man, necessarily, physically return to his real estate? The ownership of the land has changed hands, but people haven't necessarily been moved around. (For example, a man can sell his land and rent it back from the new owner, so that he continues to live on the land.) What actually happens in the Jubilee year is that the *ownership* of the field reverts to its original owner. But the verse says "each man returns to his heritage."

This is what is bothering Rashi.

How does his comment help matters?

YOUR ANSWER:

UNDERSTANDING RASHI

An Answer: Rashi tells us the underlying meaning of the Torah's words. That the ownership of the property reverts back to its original owner, not that the man physically returns to his field. When we compare this verse with the verses which speak of the freed slave returning to his family (25:41) we can be see the difference. The slave actually returns to his family; but in our verse, the man need not necessarily actually return to his land; the ownership returns to him.

A CLOSER LOOK

Notice that Rashi says "the *fields* revert to their owners."

Why didn't he use the Torah's language and say: "the heritage" reverts to their owners?

Hint: See verses 25:29, 30.

YOUR ANSWER:

A CLEARER UNDERSTANDING

An Answer: There are some heritages that do not revert to their original owner in the Jubilee year. A house in a walled city (25:29,30) may be returned to its owner *only* within the first year, if it is monetarily redeemed. Otherwise, it remains in the buyer's possession even through the Jubilee year. Thus, Rashi was careful not use the word "heritage" which would have included such houses as well. Only fields revert to their owner in Jubilee.

(See *Knizel*)

In Summary: Rashi has rephrased the Torah's message in clearer words than those of the Torah itself.

What would you ask about that?

YOUR QUESTION:

A DEEPER QUESTION_____

A Question: Why, then, didn't the Torah, itself, say (as Rashi did) "each field shall return to its owner," instead of "each man shall return to his heritage"?

Such questions are not usually asked, but they must be, if we are to fully appreciate not only Rashi's words but the Torah's words as well.

Hint: Look closely at the whole verse.

YOUR ANSWER:

A DEEPER UNDERSTANDING_____

An Answer: See the emphasis of the verse, it says:

> "You shall sanctify the fiftieth year and you shall proclaim freedom throughout the land **for all its inhabitants**; it is a Jubilee year **for you** and **you shall** return, **each man** to his heritage, and **you shall** return, **each man** to his family."

The Torah wants to emphasize the individual's freedom as a result of the Jubilee. "**All** its inhabitants" are free; some are free from financial debts, some from servitude and some from the results of their poverty, i.e., having had to sell their land and thus to be separated from their ancestral heritage. The Torah's emphasis required the phrasing "*each man* shall return" to drive home this point of individual freedom. Rashi, on the other, wanted to explain the precise meaning of these words, so he rephrased them to spell out clearly the Torah's intent.

Subtleties, subtleties, as deep as the eye can discern.

Leviticus 25:18,19

18. וַעֲשִׂיתֶם אֶת־חֻקֹּתַי וְאֶת־מִשְׁפָּטַי תִּשְׁמְרוּ וַעֲשִׂיתֶם אֹתָם וִישַׁבְתֶּם עַל־הָאָרֶץ לָבֶטַח.

19. וְנָתְנָה הָאָרֶץ פִּרְיָהּ וַאֲכַלְתֶּם לָשֹׂבַע וִישַׁבְתֶּם לָבֶטַח עָלֶיהָ.

18. וישבתם על הארץ לבטח. שבעון שמטה ישראל גולים שנאמר 'אז תרצה הארץ את שבתותיה...והרצת את שבתותיה' ושבעים שנה של גלות בבל כנגד שבעים שמטות שבטלו, היו.

19. ונתנה הארץ וגו' וישבתם לבטח עליה. שלא תדאגו משנת בצורת.

18. **And you will dwell on the Land securely.** *Rashi:* For through the sin of (not observing) the Sabbatical year, Israel is exiled, as it says: 'Then the Land will be appeased for its Sabbatical years ... and be appeased for its Sabbatical years.' The seventy years of the Babylonian exile correspond to the seventy Sabbatical years which they did not observe.

19. **The Land will give forth, etc. and you will dwell securely on it.** *Rashi:* You shall not worry about a year of famine.

WHAT IS RASHI SAYING? _____

In both of these comments Rashi is explaining the specific meaning of "security" in their respective verses.

Why need he do this?

What is bothering him?

WHAT IS BOTHERING RASHI? _____

An Answer: Verse 18 says "and you will dwell on the Land securely." Verse 19 repeats "And you will dwell securely on it." Why the repetition?

This is likely what was bothering Rashi.

How do his comments deal with this problem?

YOUR ANSWER:

UNDERSTANDING RASHI

An Answer: In the first comment "security" means being secure from fear of being evicted from the Land, if they observe the Sabbatical year. In the second comment "security" means "having enough food not to worry about a famine."

In both of these comments Rashi follows the same line of reasoning to determine what "security" means.

He sees the connection between the first half of each verse and its second half. In the first verse it says "and you shall do My statutes ...and you shall dwell on the Land securely..." In the second it says , "and the Land will give forth its fruits...and you will live securely on it." Clearly, there is a cause and effect relationship between the two halves of each verse. Keep the laws of the Sabbatical year...and you will live securely. The Land will give forth its fruit ...and you will live securely. It is a common rule of Torah interpretation, that when you have two halves to a verse, they are related in some way, either associatively or causally. The two parts of each of these verses are related one to the other, even if, at first sight, they don't seem to have any connection to each other.

A CLOSER LOOK

If we look closely at these verses we see something interesting which illustrates the Torah's precision in wording. We have already mentioned a rule in Torah interpretation which teaches us that the order of words conveys its own meaning. That means that usually the first mentioned term is the one to be emphasized. (Many examples of this can be found in my book *Studying the Torah* published by Jason Aronson.)

Now notice something interesting as we compare these two verses.

One says:

"And you will **dwell on the Land** securely."

The other says:

"you will dwell **securely** on it (the Land)."

Do you see that in the first verse "land" comes before "security"; in the second verse, "security" comes before "on it," which refers to the Land. The first verse emphasizes the point that the people will remain *on the Land*, therefore "land" comes first. Land is the point of emphasis. In the second verse, the emphasis on the productivity of the Land which is its *financial security*. Therefore this, namely the financial security (the abundance), comes before the Land is mentioned.

The Torah's subtle way of making a point is sometimes overlooked. The benefits gained by a careful reading of not only *what* the Torah says but also *how* it says it, pays off in discovering new insights and gaining a greater respect for the Torah's depth.

The Torah teaches us proper conduct in financial matters, with Rashi's help.

Leviticus 25:25

כִּי-יָמוּךְ אָחִיךָ וּמָכַר מֵאֲחֻזָּתוֹ וּבָא גֹאֲלוֹ הַקָּרֹב אֵלָיו וְגָאַל אֵת מִמְכַּר אָחִיו.

כִּי יָמוּךְ אָחִיךָ וּמָכַר. מלמד שאין אדם רשאי למכור שדהו אלא מחמת דוחק עוני.

מֵאֲחֻזָּתוֹ. ולא כולה, למד דרך ארץ שישייר שדה לעצמו.
If your brother becomes impoverished. *Rashi:* This teaches that a person is not permitted to sell his field except when under the pressure of poverty.
From his heritage. *Rashi:* But not all of it. This teaches proper conduct, that he should leave a field for himself.

These two Rashi-comments are connected. We will look at each one individually, then at them together. First, the first comment.

What would you ask about it?

YOUR QUESTION:

QUESTIONING RASHI

A Question: How does Rashi derive the rule that one must not sell his real estate unless he is impoverished? What about the verse lead him (and the *midrash*) to this conclusion?

What's bothering him?

Hint: Compare our verse with the following verses, also from this section.

"When you make a sale to your fellow or when you buy from the hand of your fellow, do not victimize one another, ..." (25:14)

" If a man shall sell a residence house in a walled city, its redemption shall be until the end of the year of its sale, ..." (25:29).

Do you see any difference between them and our verse?

What's bothering Rashi?

YOUR ANSWER:

WHAT IS BOTHERING RASHI?

An Answer: Verse 29, like our verse, also speaks of a sale; in that case, the sale of one's house. The verse says: And if a man sell a house..." and goes on to tell us how it can be redeemed. No mention is made of "If your brother becomes poor..." The reason for the man's deciding to sell his property is really irrelevant. All that concerns us are the conditions for redeeming it.

In view of this, our question is: Why does our verse mention the man's becoming impoverished? Why should the Torah tell us the man's financial condition that led him to sell? All that should concern us are the conditions for redeeming it.

This is what is bothering Rashi.

How does his comment help us?

YOUR ANSWER:

UNDERSTANDING RASHI

An Answer: His comment explains that these "irrelevant words" are really quite relevant. They teach an important rule: That "a man is only permitted to part with his ancestral heritage" if his financial misfortunes have brought him to the point of poverty.

Now let us look at Rashi's second comment.

What would you ask?

YOUR QUESTION:

QUESTIONING RASHI

A Question: How does Rashi know that a person should never sell all his property; rather he should leave at least one field for himself? What in these words lead him to that conclusion?

YOUR ANSWER:

UNDERSTANDING RASHI

An Answer: The Hebrew word here is מאחוזתו literally "**from** (i.e., *some of*) his heritage." It could have said: ומכר אחוזתו The extra מ clues us in that he hasn't sold all of his heritage.

A CLOSER LOOK

Now that we have understood both comments, let us compare them. Do you see any difference between them in the way Rashi phrases the two rules of conduct?

YOUR ANSWER:

An Answer: In the first comment, Rashi says one is "not permitted" to sell his field, unless he is impoverished. In the second comment, Rashi says it is "proper conduct" not to sell all your land. Why in one case is it "not permitted" while in the other it is only a matter of "proper conduct"?

Can you think of a reasonable answer?

YOUR ANSWER:

A CLEARER UNDERSTANDING

An Answer: If a man is not in difficult financial straits, the Torah may forbid him to sell even part of his ancestral heritage. Inasmuch as he doesn't need the money for survival there is no justifiable reason for him to sell the land of his heritage. Therefore, Rashi tells us, under such circumstances, the person should not sell his land. If, on the other hand, he needs the money to live on (which is the case in this verse), then the Torah does not prohibit selling his heritage. If this is necessary for survival, he may do so. But, Rashi tells us, it is proper conduct not to sell it off completely. It is not forbidden to do so and under particularly dire financial circumstances, he may even sell all of it. The Torah can only say that doing so isn't proper conduct and that he should do his best to avoid such an eventuality. But being a *Toras Chaim,* a "Torah of Life," it would not absolutely forbid such an act, since it enables him to live.

Rashi teaches us a lesson in Torah values in living.

Leviticus 25:41

וְיָצָא מֵעִמָּךְ הוּא וּבָנָיו עִמּוֹ וְשָׁב אֶל־מִשְׁפַּחְתּוֹ וְאֶל־אֲחֻזַּת אֲבֹתָיו יָשׁוּב.

> **וְאֶל אֲחֻזַּת אֲבֹתָיו.** אֶל כְּבוֹד אֲבֹתָיו וְאֵין לְזַלְזְלוֹ בְּכָךְ.
>
> **אֲחֻזַּת.** חֲזָקָת.
>
> **And to the heritage of his ancestors**: *Rashi:* To the dignity of his ancestors, and he is not to be demeaned by this (by the fact that he was a slave).
> **Heritage**: *Rashi:* i.e., the previous status.

There are two Rashi-comments here. Let us look at the second one.

What would you ask about Rashi's defining the word אחוזת?

Hint: Look at the previous sections of this chapter.

YOUR QUESTION:

QUESTIONING RASHI

A Question: Rashi here defines a word that has already appeared in the Torah; in fact it has appeared in this very sedra several times. (see ch.25 verses: 10, 13, 24, 25, 27, 28, 32, 33.) Yet he did not find the need to comment on this word when it appeared previously. Why now? Whenever Rashi gives the meaning of a word that has already appeared in the Torah and when it did appear he did not give its meaning, there is always room to ask: Why now and not previously? (See, for example, our analysis of "For you were strangers" Exodus 22:20 in the Shemos volume of *What's Bothering Rashi?*)

What is bothering him here?

Hint: Compare our verse with the others listed above.

YOUR ANSWER:

WHAT IS BOTHERING RASHI?

An Answer: In all the previous verses the word אחוזה had its usual connotation: real property, i.e., land. But in our verse that cannot be its meaning, since this is a case of a man who was sold into slavery. He is now being freed and returns to his family. Property has nothing to do with our case. What, then, can the word אחוזה mean here? That is what's bothering Rashi.

How does his comment deal with this?

YOUR ANSWER:

UNDERSTANDING RASHI

An Answer: Rashi makes us aware that this word can have another meaning: Status or position. The word אחוזה derives from the word אוחז which means "to hold." Thought of in this way, it is quite easy to understand that one can "hold" both a possession (land) as well as a position (status). Rashi tells us (in his previous comment) that this slave returns to his previous status, namely, that of an equal, fully entitled citizen.

Rashi says, furthermore, in the first comment, that this freed-man is not to be demeaned by the fact that he had once been a servant. He is now a free man. He has paid his debt to society, now he is returned to his previous status. His past should never be used against him.

THE LESSON

Certainly this a powerful lesson. A lesson that conveys, in a clear and unequivocal way, the dignity of man. The Torah's concern for the dignity of man, who is made in the image of G-d, comes across in the Torah many times, in many ways. An exquisite example is found in Deut. 25:3 where the Torah speaks of flogging a guilty person.

אַרְבָּעִים יַכֶּנּוּ לֹא יֹסִיף פֶּן־יֹסִיף לְהַכֹּתוֹ עַל־אֵלֶּה מַכָּה רַבָּה וְנִקְלָה
אָחִיךָ לְעֵינֶיךָ.

"Forty shall you strike him, he shall not add [to this] lest
he strike him an additional blow beyond these and *your
brother will be degraded in your eyes.*"

The words "lest ...your *brother* will be degraded in your eyes" are interpreted by Rashi (on the basis of the Sages) to mean: Once this sinner has
received his punishment, he has returned to become your "brother," your
equal, again. Don't degrade him!

Our progressive Twenty-first century society still has much to learn from
the ancient Torah regarding human dignity and how it is manifested in
our daily living. Even a man found guilty of a crime, once he has been
punished, is to be reinstated to full "brotherhood," how much more so
our fellow man who is not a sinner! So too a man who once was a servant, nevertheless, after his freedom, his slate is wiped clean; he is returned to his previous, untarnished status.

Again, we learn from Rashi to listen carefully to the Torah's words.

Leviticus 25:53

כִּשְׂכִיר שָׁנָה בְּשָׁנָה יִהְיֶה עִמּוֹ לֹא־יִרְדֶּנּוּ בְּפֶרֶךְ לְעֵינֶיךָ.

לֹא ירדנו בפרך לעיניך. כלומר ואתה רואה.

**He shall not subjugate him through harsh labor in your
sight.** *Rashi:* That is to say, and you see it.

A Rule In Rashi's Style _____

Whenever Rashi says כלומר "that is to say" he is excluding another possible, but wrong, interpretation.

Questioning Rashi _____

What is he excluding here?

Your Answer:

What Interpretation is Rashi Excluding? _____

An Answer: This is quite a subtle point. It shows us how supersensitive Rashi was to the nuances of words and to their possible overly literal interpretation. Taken literally, these words mean: You shall not allow the gentile owner to subjugate his Israelite slave in front of your eyes. The direct implication is: He may subjugate him harshly as long as it is not done in front of your eyes! But such a conclusion is certainly ridiculous. Harshly subjugating the Israelite slave is wrong whenever or wherever it is done. This incorrect implication of these words is what Rashi has come to exclude.

How do Rashi's words accomplish this?

Your Answer:

Understanding Rashi _____

An Answer: By adding the words "and you see it" Rashi tells us that witnessing this crime is a not a condition for guilt; rather it is a condition for us to interfere and stop this act. The verse, with Rashi's comment is now to be read: "As a yearly hired servant he shall be with him. He shall not rule over him with vigor while you see this, i.e., and let him get away with this behavior." Implicit is the command that you interfere and restrain the slave owner from such unwarranted and degrading behavior.

When we give this verse more thought we can better understand the thrust of this mitzvah. Compare our verse with verses 25:39 and 25:43. These verses command a Jewish master not to deal harshly with his Hebrew servant. Our verse is speaking of gentile master who owns a Hebrew servant. The Torah was given to the Jews not to the gentiles. Therefore our verse cannot be a mitzvah to a gentile master not to rule harshly with his servant; it must be a mitzvah addressed to a Jew. Therefore the Torah adds the word לעיניך emphasizing that this is a command to the Jew not to stand by idly if he sees his fellow Jew being abused by his gentile master. And this is what Rashi was also emphasizing with his words ואתה רואה, meaning the burden of responsibility is on you!

(See *Knizel*)

Rashi's brief comment leads to a surprising discovery of a hidden consistency in the Torah.

Leviticus 26:6-7

6. וְנָתַתִּי שָׁלוֹם בָּאָרֶץ וּשְׁכַבְתֶּם וְאֵין מַחֲרִיד וְהִשְׁבַּתִּי חַיָּה רָעָה מִן־הָאָרֶץ וְחֶרֶב לֹא־תַעֲבֹר בְּאַרְצְכֶם.

7. וּרְדַפְתֶּם אֶת־אֹיְבֵיכֶם וְנָפְלוּ לִפְנֵיכֶם לֶחָרֶב.

לפניכם לחרב. איש בחרב רעהו.

Before you by the sword: *Rashi:* A man by the sword of his fellow. *

WHAT IS RASHI SAYING?

This comment tells us that the enemy will kill themselves by their own "friendly fire."

What would you ask on this strange comment?

YOUR QUESTION:

QUESTIONING RASHI

A Question: An obvious question is: How does Rashi know that the enemy falls by the hand of his fellow comrade-in-arms and not, the more likely meaning, that he fell by the sword of the Israelite? What lead Rashi to this unlikely interpretation?

What's bothering Rashi here?

YOUR ANSWER:

What Is Bothering Rashi?

An Answer: Some commentators suggest that the words "before you" are superfluous. They are unnecessary since the enemy usually falls "before you." The addition of these words implies that the enemy will fall even before you get to them, i.e., by their own hand. In addition, if Israel was the cause of the enemy's falling, it should have said והפלתם "and you will fell them." The word ונפלו "and they will fall" sounds like this happened by itself, that is, felled by their own hand.

In addition to these conventional explanations, we find another, truly eye-opening, explanation for Rashi's comment.

An Amazing Answer

A brilliant answer has been suggested which shows the subtle nuances that can be uncovered in the Torah, if we only look for them. The *Nefesh Hager,* a commentary on the Targum Onkelos, points out an astounding consistency throughout the Tanach: Whenever the Tanach speaks of Jews (or G-d) waging war and killing non-Jews, the words used are לפי חרב. However, whenever gentiles (or G-d) are described as killing the Jews, the words consistently used are לחרב or בחרב.

Some examples of the former can be found in: Genesis 34:26; Numbers 21:24; Joshua 8:24.

Some examples of the latter can be found in: Exodus 3:13; 22:23; Numbers 14:43; 20:18; Psalms 78:62.

Since our verse uses the word לחרב (and not לפי חרב) even though the Israelites are battling the gentiles and לפי חרב would be appropriate, this indicates that the gentiles are the ones who are doing the killing! "Each by the sword of the other."

What Does לפי חרב Mean?

What sense can be made out of this linguistic consistency? Why would the Tanach differentiate between the use of the word לחרב "by the sword" and לפי חרב "by the blade of the sword"? A little thought should give you the answer.

Hint: See Genesis 48:22 where Jacob tells Joseph that he took the city of Shechem בחרבי ובקשתי (literally "with my sword and bow") and Rashi's comment there.

An Answer: In Genesis 48:22 Rashi translates בחרבי ובקשתי as "with wisdom
and prayer." On the basis of that comment we can conclude that
when the Jew wages war he precedes his battle with prayer to the
Almighty. This, then, may be the symbolic meaning of the phrase
לפי חרב which is usually translated as "by the blade of the sword"
but which literally means "by the mouth of the sword." The mouth
(prayer) always precedes the sword in battles waged by Jews!

(See *Nefesh Hager*)

In (spiritual) numbers there is (military) strength.

Leviticus 26:8

וְרָדְפוּ מִכֶּם חֲמִשָּׁה מֵאָה וּמֵאָה מִכֶּם רְבָבָה יִרְדֹּפוּ וְנָפְלוּ אֹיְבֵיכֶם
לִפְנֵיכֶם לֶחָרֶב.

חמשה...מאה ומאה מכם רבבה. וכי כך החשבון? והלא לא היה
צריך לומר אלא ומאה מכם שני אלפים ירדופו? אלא אינו
דומה מועטין העושין את התורה למרובין העושין את התורה.
**Five... one hundred; and one hundred of you, ten thou-
sand.** *Rashi*: Is this the correct calculation? Should it not
have rather said 'and a hundred from among you will
pursue two thousand'? But you cannot compare a few
who fulfill the Torah to the many who fulfill the Torah.

What Is Rashi Saying?

Rashi asks his question quite openly in this comment, no need to guess
what it is. A simple calculation shows that we have a discrepancy here.
If five will pursue one hundred, that means that every Israelite soldier
will pursue twenty of the enemy. So, likewise, a hundred Israelite soldiers should pursue two thousand of the enemy, which is twenty times
one hundred, and not the much larger number of ten thousand.

Why then does the Torah say "ten thousand"?

Rashi asks and answers, as well.

His answer is that in numbers there is strength. So if a hundred Jewish
solders, who keep the Torah, fight the enemy, their overall effect is of
greater proportional power than if a fewer number of solders did battle.
Their effect is increased geometrically, not arithmetically.

The meaning is clear enough, but there is still room to ask.

What would you ask?

YOUR QUESTION:

QUESTIONING RASHI

A Question: The question about proportions is clear but why does Rashi say "the few who keep the Torah"? Why mention the Torah? Maybe the message of these disproportionate numbers is simply that "in numbers there is strength" with or without Torah observance?

YOUR ANSWER:

UNDERSTANDING RASHI

An Answer: This whole chapter is a blessing and a curse. The blessing (of plentitude, pursuing one's enemies and finally, peace) comes as a reward for "If you will go in My decrees and observe My commandments (26:3). In short, observing the Torah is the condition for receiving G-d's rewards, and military success is one of these rewards. This is certainly Rashi's intent.

THE *MIZRACHI'S* QUESTION ON RASHI

Rav Eliyahu Mizrachi, one the foremost commentators on Rashi, asks the following question:

What would Rashi say about the verse in Deut. 32:30:

אֵיכָה יִרְדֹּף אֶחָד אֶלֶף וּשְׁנַיִם יָנִיסוּ רְבָבָה...

"How could one pursue a thousand and two cause ten thousand to flee."

Here too we have a disproportionate increase, one pursuing a thousand should extrapolate to two pursuing two thousand, not, as the Torah says here, ten thousand. But this verse is referring to the pagan gentiles pursuing the Jews. Certainly they can't be credited with "the many observing the Torah"! Therefore, says, the *Mizrachi,* the reasonable explanation for the disproportionate increase, both for the Children of Israel and for the gentiles, is the known fact that "in numbers there is strength," irregardless of the observance of the Torah.

Can you think of a defense of Rashi? Why do you think Rashi's comment is appropriate on our verse but not on the verse in Deuteronomy ?

YOUR ANSWER:

In Defense of Rashi

An Answer: The *Gur Aryeh* points out an obvious difference between our verse and the verse in Deuteronomy which speaks of the gentiles pursuing the Jews. There it says "How could one *pursue* a thousand and two cause ten thousand *to flee.*"

Notice there is no parallelism here, as there is in our verse. Two may cause ten thousand *to flee.* Causing the enemy to flee is not the same as pursuing them. It is quite reasonable that it would take fewer men to cause a larger group to flee, than to actually, physically, pursue them. Therefore, the disproportionate increase is due to the differnt actions the soldiers are doing. While in our verse there is an exact parallel, both groups are pursuing — five are pursuing a hundred and a hundred are pursuing ten thousand.

(See *Mizrachi, Gur Aryeh*)

Rashi's *Midrashic* Source

Rashi makes a slight change when he quotes the *midrash*. Can you spot it?

The *midrash* of *Toras Cohanim* says:

ומאה מכם רבבה – וכי כך הוא החשבון? והלא לא היה צריך
לומר אלא 'מאה מכם שני אלפים ירדופו'? אלא אין דומה
המרובים העושים את התורה למועטים העושים את התורה.

What change did Rashi make?

YOUR ANSWER:

An Answer: The *midrash* says "*Many* who fulfill the Torah cannot be compared to a *few* who fulfill the Torah." While Rashi says "The *few* who fulfill the Torah cannot be compared to the *many* who fulfill the Torah."

Rashi reverses the saying. Considering that Rashi quoted each word from the *midrash* exactly, except for this phrase, this change cannot be ascribed to his poor memory. He must have done this intentionally. Why?

YOUR ANSWER:

RASHI'S CHANGE

An Answer: It is important to notice this slight change, because it shows how precise Rashi is in his work. Since Rashi's task, as Torah commentator, is to explain the verse, he follows the order of the verse. The verse first mentions the few, then it mentions the many. So too does Rashi. He first mentions the "few who fulfill the Torah" then the "many who fulfill the Torah." The *midrash*, on the other hand, is interested in teaching us the principle of the importance of observing the Torah and its rewards, therefore it placed first the many, in order to emphasize this.

THE LESSON

When Rashi re-words a *midrash* or changes it in any way, it is cause for examination. He does so intentionally.

Rashi again draws from the midrash but makes slight changes.

Leviticus 26:42

וְזָכַרְתִּי אֶת־בְּרִיתִי יַעֲקוֹב וְאַף אֶת־בְּרִיתִי יִצְחָק וְאַף אֶת־בְּרִיתִי אַבְרָהָם אֶזְכֹּר וְהָאָרֶץ אֶזְכֹּר.

וזכרתי את ברית יעקוב. למה נמנו אחורנית? כלומר כדאי הוא יעקב הקטן לכך, ואם אינו כדאי הרי יצחק עמו, ואם אינו כדאי הרי אברהם עמו שהוא כדאי. ולמה לא נאמרה זכירה ביצחק? אלא אפרו של יצחק נראה לפני צבור ומונח על המזבח.

I will remember My covenant with Jacob. *Rashi:* Why are they listed backwards? As if to say: Jacob, the youngest, is worthy of that; and if he is not worthy, behold, Isaac is with him, and if he is not worthy, behold, Abraham is with him and he is worthy. And why is the word "remembrance" not mentioned in connection with Isaac? Since the ashes of Isaac (from the *Akeidah)* are seen before me piled up and placed on the altar.

WHAT IS RASHI SAYING?

Clearly what is disturbing Rashi is the backward listing of the Fathers. Everywhere else in the Torah they are listed as Abraham, Isaac and Jacob, why is it otherwise here?

Rashi tells us the logic behind this backward order. The merits of the Fathers are mentioned here as justification for saving the people from total destruction, even though the people may deserve their punishment. The Torah seems to imply that perhaps if their sins are not too bad, then Jacob's merits alone can save them. But even if the sins are more grievous, then Isaac's merits together with Jacob's are needed to save them. And if the worst is anticipated, and Jacob and Isaac are not sufficient protection, then Abraham's merits can also be added to the scales. This will certainly be sufficient.

Let us look at Rashi's *midrashic* source and compare his comment with it.

RASHI'S *MIDRASHIC* SOURCE

Rashi's source is the *midrash* in *Vayikra Rabbah*. There it says:

"Why are the Fathers listed backwards? To say: If the acts of Jacob are not worthy, the acts of Isaac are worthy, and if the acts of Isaac are not worthy, the acts of Abraham are worthy. The acts of *each one* is sufficiently worthy that the world can be saved for his sake."

You see that Rashi's comment is somewhat different from the *midrash's* words.

What has he changed and Why?

First, what changes do you see?

YOUR ANSWER:

RASHI'S CHANGES

An Answer: The main difference seems to be that while the *midrash* summarizes by saying that the acts of *each alone* should be sufficiently worthy to save the world. Rashi leaves this out.

What might be an explanation for this?

YOUR ANSWER:

UNDERSTANDING RASHI'S CHANGES

An Answer: The verse says "I will remember My covenant with Jacob *and also* My covenant with Isaac *and also* My covenant with Abraham will I remember..." We see that the verse does not take each Father separately but cumulatively, "*and also* My covenant with..." This may be the reason that Rashi preferred to see the cumulative effects of the merits of the Fathers as opposed to their individual merits, as the *midrash* did.

The latter part of this comment also comes from *Vayikra Rabbah*. The *midrash* says:

"Why does it say remembrance by Jacob and by Abraham but not by Isaac? Rav Brechya said: Because he suffered from afflictions (i.e., he was blind). The Rabbis said: He saw the ashes of Isaac as if they were piled up the altar."

We see that Rashi chose the Rabbis' interpretation over that of Rav Brechya's.

Can you see what might have guided Rashi in this choice?

YOUR ANSWER:

An Answer: When Rashi uses *drash* he strives to use those that are closest to *p'shat*. The Rabbis' *drash* here explains why G-d did not need a remembrance for Isaac — because his ashes were in front of Him all the time. Rav Brechya's *drash,* on the other hand, doesn't deal as directly with the issue of remembrance.

A CLOSER LOOK

Did you notice that it says "the ashes of Isaac" This refers to the sacrifice of Isaac by Abraham (the *Akaidah*). But in the end, Isaac was not sacrificed! There were no ashes! Yet here it says "the ashes of Isaac." Why?

This would seem to be the *midrash's* way of saying: Abraham and Isaac's intentions were so sincere, that G-d considered it as if they had, in actuality, gone through with the sacrifice.

Rashi and *P'shat*

Rashi has made use of the Sage's *drash* to explain the unusual order of the listing of the Fathers in this verse. It is a comment that exists somewhere on the continuum between *p'shat* and *drash*.

For an original *p'shat* interpretation of this problem, we can look to an early commentator, Rav Yosef Bechor Shor, one of the *Ba'alei HaTosephos*, born a hundred years after Rashi. He says, that since we are speaking of G-d remembering the Fathers, and since Jacob, was the last of the Fathers, he is nearest in time to the present. Therefore, it would be easiest (in human terms) to remember him. Thus, *Hashem* says I will remember Jacob and, if necessary, I will even remember the more remote Isaac, and, if necessary, I will remember even the furthest back in time, Abraham.

Of course, while G-d's "memory" is not affected by time, nevertheless, the verse refers to His memory and inasmuch as "the Torah speaks in the language of man" this interpretation is a most reasonable *p'shat* explanation for the reversed order.

Yet Rashi has chosen the way of the Sages to combine *p'shat* and *drash*. This point is rarely understood but important to make: while Rashi establishes *p'shat* as a central feature of his commentary, nevertheless his version of *p'shat* is strongly influenced by the Sages' *midrashic* interpretations. Frequently the Ramban will argue with Rashi regarding points of *p'shat* such as these.

(See *Bechor Shor*)

A classic example of Rashi's ingenious eye-opening interpretative skills. This comment reveals Rashi's true genius.

Leviticus 26:44

וְאַף גַּם־זֹאת בִּהְיוֹתָם בְּאֶרֶץ אֹיְבֵיהֶם לֹא־מְאַסְתִּים וְלֹא־גְעַלְתִּים לְכַלֹּתָם לְהָפֵר בְּרִיתִי אִתָּם כִּי אֲנִי הֹ' אֱלֹקֵיהֶם.

וְאַף גַּם זֹאת. וְאַף אֲפִילוּ אֲנִי עוֹשֶׂה עִמָּהֶם זֹאת הַפּוּרְעָנוּת אֲשֶׁר אָמַרְתִּי בִּהְיוֹתָם בְּאֶרֶץ אוֹיְבֵיהֶם לֹא אֶמְאָסֵם לְכַלּוֹתָם וּלְהָפֵר בְּרִיתִי אֲשֶׁר אִתָּם.

And yet for all this: *Rashi*: But also even if I shall execute upon them this punishment which I mentioned, when they shall be in the land of their enemies, I will not despise them to make an end to them and to make void my covenant which is with them.

Before we analyze this apparently simple, but actually highly complex, comment, let us first see what Rashi has done.

WHAT HAS RASHI DONE?

Rashi has rephrased the Torah's words. There are many questions that can be asked here. But first let us see what rephrasing Rashi has done.

What changes has he made?

How many of Rashi's changes and insertions can you point out?

YOUR ANSWER:

RASHI'S CHANGES

An Answer: To better see these changes, we will set the Torah's words (in Hebrew) opposite Rashi's.

The Torah's words	Rashi's words
וְאַף גַּם	וְאַף אֲפִילוּ
——————	אֲנִי עוֹשֶׂה עִמָּהֶם
זֹאת	זֹאת הַפּוּרְעָנוּת
——————	אֲשֶׁר אָמַרְתִּי
בִּהְיוֹתָם בְּאֶרֶץ אוֹיְבֵיהֶם	בִּהְיוֹתָם בְּאֶרֶץ אוֹיְבֵיהֶם

The Torah's words	Rashi's words
לא מאסתים ולא געלתים לכלתם	לא אמאסם לכלתם
להפר בריתי	ולהפר בריתי
אתם	אשר אתם

You know Rashi by now, so you realize that not one of these changes is for naught. Our job, after noting them, is to understand the reason for them. Several things are bothering Rashi and because of them he made these changes.

QUESTIONING RASHI

A Question: Why has Rashi made these revisions?

What are the things that are bothering him?

YOUR ANSWER:

WHAT *ARE* BOTHERING RASHI?

Answer: 1) Both words אף and גם mean "also." Why the redundancy?

2) The word זאת is unnecessary. Remove it and you will see that the verse would have the same meaning as it does with it.

2a) As a matter of fact, each of these three words are unnecessary. The verse could just as well have said: "When they will be in the land of their enemies, I will not abhor them nor will I reject them etc." Nothing is lost by eliminating these first three words of the verse. Rashi is implicitly asking: Why are they here?

3) When we read this verse, it seems to say: " G-d will not destroy the people, *that is to say*, to void His covenant with them." Certainly that makes no sense! G-d's covenant with His people was not merely a promise not to destroy them; it was much more than that. It was a promise of receiving the land of Canaan. But our verse clearly says: "I will not despise them to destroy them, to break My covenant with them."

That verse equates not destroying them with not breaking the covenant.

How have Rashi's changes improved matters?

YOUR ANSWERS:

Understanding Rashi's Changes

1) Rashi reinterprets the word גם to mean "even" (see for example Jeremiah 2:33) and not "also." Sometimes, albeit rarely, it carries this meaning. With this change, there is no redundancy.

2) Rashi rephrases the word זאת to mean "*this* punishment which I have said."

On what authority does he do this? We already noted that the word is unnecessary, but how does Rashi know it refers to a "punishment which I have said"? Rashi points the way to understanding by adding the words "which I (i.e., *Hashem*) said." What is Rashi referring to?

Hint: Review the section of the curse.

A *Giveaway Hint*: Do you see the word זאת previously in this chapter?

YOUR ANSWER:

The Depth of Rashi

An Answer: Of course the word זאת is found; it even occurs twice.

* In Leviticus 26:16 at the very beginning of the description of the punishments:

אַף־אֲנִי אֶעֱשֶׂה־**זֹּאת** לָכֶם וְהִפְקַדְתִּי עֲלֵיכֶם בֶּהָלָה אֶת־הַשַּׁחֶפֶת וְאֶת־ הַקַּדַּחַת מְכַלּוֹת עֵינַיִם וּמְדִיבֹת נָפֶשׁ וגו'

* A second time we find this word, in Leviticus 26: 27...41:

וְאִם־בְּ**זֹאת** לֹא תִשְׁמְעוּ לִי...וְהֵבֵאתִי אֹתָם בְּאֶרֶץ אֹיְבֵיהֶם וגו'

Note something important. The first verse introduces the section of punishments which will befall the people while they continue to live in the land, before they are exiled. The second verse introduces the punishments which will befall them when they are exiled from the land, "in the land of their enemies."

We now can see that the word זאת in this section connotes punishment. The word זאת is a code word! Rashi understood this and he clued us into it. This is what Rashi means when he says "the punishments *which I said*." Now look again at Rashi's words. What does he add after "the punishments which I said"?

He adds: "while you are in the land of your enemies." This is one of Rashi's neat techniques. He clarifies something and at the same time uses the Torah's own words. His clarification is that the זאת referred to here is the second one, the one that introduces the punishment of exile. And he says this by interweaving his words with the Torah's words.

זאת הפורענות אשר אמרתי **בהיותם בארץ אויביהם**.

Compare Rashi's words the Torah's word in 26:27...34:

וְאִם־**בְּזֹאת** לֹא תִשְׁמְעוּ לִי...**וְהֵבֵאתִי אֹתָם בְּאֶרֶץ אֹיְבֵיהֶם** וְגוֹ׳

The Torah has subtly connected our verse with the previous section by the technique of word-association of the word זאת. Rashi worded his comment here in such a way as to make us aware of that word association.

We should pause a moment to take stock of this ingenious interpretation and make note of the brilliance of Rashi's work. By clueing us in to the hidden meaning and significance of the word זאת, Rashi has opened our eyes to a point we never would have noticed otherwise. We see here not only the precision of each and every one of Rashi's words, we see also the sublime subtlety of the Torah's use of words.

3) By adding the letter ו to the word להפר Rashi deals with the problem of equating the covenant with not destroying the people. Rashi tells us that the verse means that *Hashem* will *not* destroy the people *nor* will he void His covenant with them. Two separate promises are made here, the covenant is separate from the promise not to destroy the nation. This is so because the covenant is much more than just that, it is the promise to give Land of Israel to the children of Abraham, Isaac and Jacob. That covenant too, *Hashem* promises, will not be annulled.

We have one last revision to deal with. Rashi inserts the word אשר.

להפר בריתי **אשר** אתם.

Can you think why he does this?

YOUR ANSWER:

An Answer: This slight change is characteristic of Rashi's precise style. He is very sensitive to syntax. "To break the covenant with them" could be misinterpreted to mean "to break the covenant *together* with (breaking) them!" By adding the word אשר, there is no longer any chance of misunderstanding, however slight that chance may have been.

THE TORAH'S POETICALLY CONSOLING MESSAGE

This verse, together with Rashi's sensitive interpretation of it, points out the powerful underlying message of the *Tochachah* — the Curse. When you read the whole curse 26:16-through our verse, you can't miss the obvious parallel, measure-for-measure method of divine retribution: G-d's punishment parallels Israel's sins. This is hammered home with the repetitive phrase: "If you walk contrary to Me, then I too will walk contrary to you" (26:24, and 26:28 and again 26:40).

Yet when we come to our verse which is the final statement of this horrific Curse, we find a unexpected tournabout. The parallelism no longer holds up. Compare these nearly parallel verses:

Leviticus 26:15:

וְאִם־בְּחֻקֹּתַי תִּמְאָסוּ וְאִם אֶת־מִשְׁפָּטַי תִּגְעַל נַפְשְׁכֶם לְבִלְתִּי עֲשׂוֹת אֶת־כָּל־מִצְוֹתַי לְהַפְרְכֶם אֶת־בְּרִיתִי.

And our verse, Leviticus 26:44

וְאַף גַּם־זֹאת בִּהְיוֹתָם בְּאֶרֶץ אֹיְבֵיהֶם לֹא־מְאַסְתִּים וְלֹא־גְעַלְתִּים לְכַלֹּתָם לְהָפֵר בְּרִיתִי אִתָּם כִּי אֲנִי הי אֱלֹקֵיהֶם.

Whereas the people had *despised* G-d's statutes and His laws were *loathed* by them and they tried to *break their covenant with G-d* (26:15), *Hashem* in direct opposition to this, makes a point of *not* paralleling their behavior. "And even when they are in the land of their enemies I will *not despise them* and I will *not loathe them*...and will *not break My covenant* with them..."

When we absorb the full significance of this analysis, we realize that the three words — וְאַף גַם זֹאת — which we had thought were superfluous, are precisely the words that carry this powerful message. The verse now is to be read as:

"But also even if I shall execute this (measure-for-measure punishment)...I will not (continue to punish them measure-for-measure and) despise them etc."

This is the essence of the unique and everlasting Covenant between G-d and His people; it is stronger and more enduring than any wayward behavior, however abhorrent, that the Israelites might do.

Hashem's message: Israel may be terribly punished by Me, but My Covenant will never be broken; My promise to the Fathers will be fulfilled — after all is said and done, the people will return to their Land.

A mighty message and a most elegant way of conveying it. All becomes clear with Rashi's help.

(See *Silbermann*)

❖❖❖

About the Author

Avigdor Bonchek has Rabbinic ordination from Ner Israel Rabbinical College of Baltimore and a doctorate in clinical psychology from New York University. He has taught Torah studies at the Ohr Somayach Center for Judaic Studies in Jerusalem. He has been a lecturer of psychological courses at the Hebrew University of Jerusalem for the past 25 years. Previously he taught at the City University of New York, Yeshiva University and Ben Gurion University in Israel. Dr. Bonchek is a practicing psychotherapist. His book *The Problem Student: A Cognitive/Behavioral Approach* has been published in Hebrew. His book *Studying the Torah: A Guide to In-Depth Interpretation* has been published by Jason Aronson Publishers. Dr. Bonchek lives in Jerusalem with his wife, Shulamis, and their six children.